Lawns and Ground Cover

ROYAL HORTICULTURAL SOCIETY

Lawns and Ground Cover

Simon Akeroyd

DK

LONDON, NEW YORK, MUNICH,
MELBOURNE, DELHI

PROJECT EDITOR Becky Shackleton
PROJECT ART EDITOR Rebecca Tennant
SENIOR EDITOR Zia Allaway
MANAGING EDITORS Esther Ripley, Penny Warren
MANAGING ART EDITOR Alison Donovan
PRODUCTION EDITOR Andy Hilliard

RHS EDITORS James Armitage, Simon Maughan
RHS PUBLISHER Rae Spencer-Jones

PHOTOGRAPHERS Peter Anderson, Brian North

First published in Great Britain in 2012 by
Dorling Kindersley Limited
80 Strand, London WC2R 0RL
Penguin Group (UK)

2 4 6 8 10 9 7 5 3 1
001-181831-Feb/2012

A CIP catalogue record for this book is available
from the British Library.

ISBN 978-1-4053-7616-7

Printed and bound by Star Standard Industries Pte Ltd,
Singapore

To find out more about RHS membership, contact:
RHS Membership Department
PO Box 313, London SW1P 2PE
Telephone: 0845 130 4646
www.rhs.org.uk

Discover more at
www.dk.com

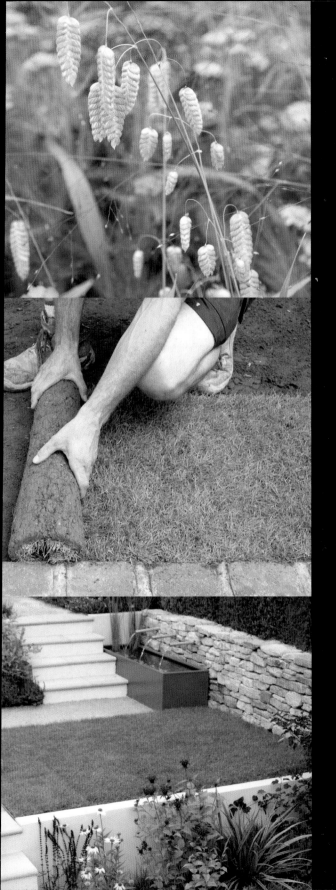

Contents

Simon Akeroyd is the Garden and
Countryside Manager at Polesden Lacey, Surrey
and was previously a Garden Manager for the RHS.
He has worked as a BBC horticultural researcher
and journalist. He is the author of *Simple Steps
Shrubs and Small Trees* and the co-author of *The
Allotment Handbook* and *Grow Your Own Fruit.*

Covering the ground

Designed to inspire you, this chapter contains bold designs and gorgeous gardens that will encourage you to think creatively when filling your outside spaces. Lawns are the obvious choice for covering large areas as they offer a lush, green surface, are cheap in comparison to man-made materials, and provide a soft space to play or relax on. However there is also a wide range of ground-cover and meadow plants that are well worth considering, offering a variety of colours, textures, and scents, which make a striking alternative to grass.

Formal swards

Highly manicured lawns may require a high degree of maintenance, but the effect can be stunning. In these gardens, the formal lawn is the centrepiece around which the rest of the design flows.

Pictures clockwise from top right

Geometric patterns The central feature of this formal design is a line of lawn squares that lead up to three turf-lined steps. Breaking up the grass with pebble pathways gives the effect of elongating the garden, making the space feel larger than it really is. The green squares of lawn are framed by formal blocks of muted, soft yellow and blue herbaceous plants, which complement them. The garden is attractively framed with regimented, pleached lime trees along the side.

Framing with topiary One of the best reasons to use lawns in a garden design is that they have the ability to unify areas of the garden, giving outdoor spaces a constancy and allowing a garden to flow from one area of interest to another. In this garden, grass is used as both a pathway leading to the sundial focal point, but also as a wider expanse of lawn in the background. The topiaried box hedges frame the space and give it symmetry.

Bordered lawn This garden uses a striking striped formal lawn as the centrepiece of the design. The curved shape is bordered with traditional cottage garden plants that help to showcase the grass to its best advantage. The circular design is echoed by the curve of the rustic walls while the wider than average stripes on the lawn give the garden a sense of width. The long meadow grass in the background highlights the difference between the formality within the design and the informality outside the walled space.

Formal focal points The stripes on this lawn lead the eye to the end of the garden where the impressive water feature forms the focal point. Formal lawns are nearly always symmetrical and the stripes create the illusion that the lawn is longer than it actually is. The flowerbeds are traditional mixed borders with drifts of planting, both framing and contrasting with the formality of the grass. The grass of a formal lawn like this would need to be cut at least twice a week with a high quality cylinder mower.

Family lawns

An essential part of any family garden, a lawn provides an ideal surface for children to play on. You needn't compromise on style though – choose a hard-wearing grass type for a durable, child-friendly space that will look good all year round.

Pictures clockwise from opposite

Play time Strong design principles are just as important in a children's play area as in ornamental gardens. This rustic swing adds height to the garden and acts as a focal point while the planting of tough, evergreen shrubs softens the hard edges of the sandpit and fence panels – choose resilient plants that will tolerate stray footballs or discarded toys. Children's play areas need tough, hard-wearing grass mixes – usually composed of rye grasses and smooth-stalked meadow grass – to be able to withstand the constant wear and tear.

Grass patterns Demonstrating that gardens can be fun as well as attractive, this unusual design encourages children and adults to make the most of the entire garden by following the looping path to the seating area. The fun pattern divides up the lawn into irregular shapes and creates interesting spaces for children to play in.

Dining spaces Creating "outdoor rooms" that adults and children can enjoy together is one of the most important elements to consider in a family garden; this al fresco dining area is one such example. Ideally, tables and chairs should be kept off the lawn as they can damage the grass, while the damp can cause the legs of wooden garden furniture to rot. As can be seen here, outside dining spaces are best situated on patios as this saves having to lift heavy furniture every time the grass needs cutting.

Fun but practical This garden combines practical functionality with contemporary design. The stylish central lawn is large and hard-wearing and its chic border, containing heucheras and ornamental grasses, contrasts attractively with it. The smooth rubber crumb path is ideal for children to ride their bikes on and wide enough for good access to the sculptured play den and the storage and seating chest, but its striking colour makes it an exciting feature in its own right.

Artificial turf

Artificial turf has many benefits: it doesn't need mowing, watering, or feeding, it's green all year round, and it can be as soft as real grass. From a distance it can be difficult to tell the real from the fake.

Pictures clockwise from top right

Eating out Dining al fresco is one of the pleasures of having a garden and there are many benefits to using artificial grass to carpet outdoor dining spaces. In this chic, modern design the sharp square of artificial grass complements the style of the furniture and will be able to withstand chairs being moved back and forth across it – unlike real grass, the high volume of footfall won't wear it away. Artificial turf is a good choice here as it won't stay moist like a natural lawn, so furniture shouldn't rust or rot and as the grass doesn't need mowing, the heavy furniture won't have to be moved each week in summer.

Kids' play area Lawns can take a real battering in areas of the garden that children regularly play in and may often need repairing or patching up. By using artificial grass instead, this garden looks fun and enticing for children yet will be robust enough to stand up to games, sports, and general wear and tear. Another great advantage is that the surface won't get muddy so children are less likely to traipse dirt into the house.

Edging Proving that edges don't have to be straight and unimaginative, this artificial lawn looks stylish and contemporary thanks to the pattern of the irregularly sized white paving blocks. One of the benefits of using artificial turf is that it will always look neat and tidy and won't require the weekly chore of edging that would be necessary with living turf.

Balconies and terraces In this contemporary design the artificial grass looks natural and vibrant and is an attractive alternative to decking or slabs. Artificial grass is ideal if you're short on space as there's no need to find space to store a mower. Living grass would struggle here due to the shade cast by the surrounding buildings, the trees in pots, and the trellis system, and would also require about 10cm (4in) of topsoil, which may put the structure of the building under significant pressure.

Sculpted turf

Grasses are versatile as well as beautiful and with a bit of imagination they can be used to reshape landscapes, create upright focal points, and used to form exciting and intriguing sculptures.

Pictures clockwise from top right

Artificial hollows This contemporary design uses artificial turf to create a rolling, undulating landscape – this material is ideal for creating complicated designs or shapes, which would prove extremely difficult to mow if created with turf. The design revolves around oppositions: the architectural shape of the upright sculptures and the perfectly straight lines of the background hedge contrast with the gentle curves and hollows. Green is the dominant colour within the design and has been used to striking effect, complemented with splashes of bright red.

Chamomile seat There are many alternatives to grass when creating a natural sculpture. In this design a usable sofa has been shaped out of the evergreen plants box and ivy while the seating area is covered with the creeping plant chamomile, which makes an ideal choice as it releases a wonderful apple scent when its leaves are crushed.

Curved bank One of the many advantages of using grass in contemporary garden design is its ability to mould to any contour whether it be vertical or horizontal. In this garden design, soil has been shaped into a raised, curved bank, or "bund", creating an enclosed central space. Meadow grasses have been sown on the top of it and then a range of small ground-cover and succulent plants have been selected to hug the inside curve and provide some colour.

Grass sculptures Many lawn grasses can be used to clothe abstract shapes due to their creeping, fast-growing habits. In this design, cuboid, pyramidal, and spherical shapes have been covered with grasses to create a cluster of upright sculptures. Several of these shapes conceal fountains – water spouts out of their tops and runs down the sides, preventing the grasses from drying out and creating a verdant, lush, contemporary effect. Grass species suitable for shady sites should be chosen for the sides facing away from the sun and the turf would need to be replaced regularly to keep it looking fresh.

Mixing and matching textures

Using contrasting elements within one design can highlight the beauty of both: these designs demonstrate that foliage, grasses, flowers, and hard landscaping can look at their most exciting when used in creative combinations with each other.

Pictures clockwise from opposite

Formal contrasts Informal drifts of meadow-like long grass and flowering borders make an attractive contrast to this garden's closely mown pathway. The longer grass should not be a vigorous type and any that overhangs the path will need to be cut back regularly, otherwise it will kill the short grass – this will then look unattractive in winter when the taller plants die back and expose it. The path will need regular mowing.

Raised turf This design contrasts colours, shapes, and textures to striking effect. The formal squares of lawn are raised on blocky slate structures and are surrounded with a soft floral display of pink bedding flowers – as though the grass and bedding have swapped places. The pencil-shaped evergreen cypress trees create upright punctuation within the design and offer an extra textural quality to the space.

Clumps of ground cover The soft, crinkled foliage and lime-green colour of these tiny, clump-forming alpines form a lovely textural contrast with the blades of grass in the lawn and the large, strap-like plants in the background. The tiny white flowers add additional interest to the border, making the alpines look like floral pincushions among the other plants.

Geometric cubes This unusual, abstract design features turf cut into a square geometric patchwork and wire cubes that have been covered with the spreading ground-cover plant mind-your-own-business (*Soleirolia soleirolii*). Its tiny foliage creates an interesting patchwork when contrasted with the blades of grass in the lawn. Mind-your-own-business will form dense carpets of matted foliage and will scramble over the wire framework and bricks. Although it can tolerate sun or shade it prefers moist conditions and therefore needs frequent watering until established.

Flowers in grass

Using flowers and grasses in contrasting colours and textures looks attractive over large areas or in pots or borders. Plant bulbs in a lawn for a spring display or let the lawn grow long and enhance it with wildflowers for a meadow effect. Prairie-style planting is quite different and takes this contrast to the extreme: mix swathes of grasses with perennials in large borders.

Pictures clockwise from top right

Contemporary combinations The foliage of the feather grass (*Stipa tenuissima*) breaks up the clumps of white roses, purple pin cushions (*Scabiosa columbaria*), and chocolate cosmos (*Cosmos atrosanguineus*), to form an open, looser style of planting that gives a modern twist to an otherwise traditional border. Ornamental grasses can be used to great effect in borders as their foliage and seedheads create an attractive contrast with the colourful flowers.

Annual meadows The most popular annual meadow flowers include poppies, daisies, and cornflowers, which also look effective on a small scale when sown into borders or flowerbeds. Meadows sown with annual flowers create a huge splash of colour in a small amount of time. If they are left to form seedheads before being cut down in late summer they should produce flowers year after year.

Prairie style This traditional prairie planting consists of fiery *Achillea* and *Rudbeckia* and airy *Stipa tenuissima*, which creates movement as it sways in the wind. Influenced by the North American prairies, this style is popular due to its spectacular display of brightly coloured flowers, low maintenance, and drought tolerance. Unlike most meadows, prairies generally contain more flowers than grass and can provide year-round interest as the plants can be left to form seedheads which look spectacular covered in frost in winter.

Spring appeal Rows of naturalized grape hyacinths (*Muscari*), *Anemone*, and *Chionodoxa* create a simple yet stunning formal effect, adding interest to this large expanse of grass. This effect can be achieved on any size lawn, using different bulbs, colours, and planting patterns. The lawn around the bulbs will need to be cut weekly in spring to retain the definition between grass and flowers.

Ground cover alternatives to grass

If you do not fancy getting the lawnmower out each week, there are many other exciting plants that can be used as an alternative to grass. Some produce masses of tiny flowers while others provide scent and attractive foliage.

Pictures clockwise from top left

Ground-cover patchwork Reminiscent of a collection of fields from the air, this striking design uses solid blocks of ground-cover plants in silver, gold, and varying shades of green to create a patchwork effect. The plants are divided and bordered by closely clipped box hedges, which as well as separating the sections, help to highlight the array of contrasting textures.

Filling the gaps Ground-cover plants such as mind-your-own-business can be used to fill gaps in patios or between stepping stones. Choose spreading or creeping species and they will establish quickly. The best type of plants to use are those that release scent when walked on such as thyme, chamomile, or Corsican mint. These plants have the attraction of giving a rustic, naturalistic feel to paving, break up the harsh lines of a pathway or patio, and give a sense of maturity to a garden.

Contrasting chamomile This garden is a modern take on the traditional Edwardian chamomile lawn, using modern hard landscaping materials and a striking, simple pattern. The white blockwork contrasts with the green foliage, giving a very clean, formal effect. Chamomile will only tolerate a modest amount of walking on and needs free-draining soil to grow successfully.

Thyme lawn This beautiful bed of thyme consists of a number of different cultivars planted in clumps to create a patchwork of colours. This bed is surrounded by an attractive curved brick edge that contains the spreading habit of the plants. Bees love this plant so do not walk across the lawn with bare feet while it is in flower. Although thyme lawns release a beautiful scent when walked on, they don't tolerate much footfall, and will benefit from having stepping stones placed through them if a lot of wear and tear is expected.

How to sow, plant, and lay turf

The key to successful gardening is nearly always in the preparation. Use this chapter to help you plan and design your garden: make a feature of your lawn and make the most of problem areas, such as under trees, next to fences, or on banks, by covering them with ground-cover plants. Then assess your site and soil so that you can choose the right plants for your garden's conditions. Finally, the simple step-by-step guide will show you how to prepare the ground thoroughly. Follow this chapter's other step-by-step guides to learn how to sow grass seed, lay turf, or plant ground cover.

Designing and planning lawns

Lawns are often the central and largest feature in a garden, so think carefully about the size and shape you want when creating a garden plan. Consider its uses, as this will determine the layout and also the type of grass you will need.

Space for everyone This clever design allows the different areas of the garden to interact with each other while also dividing them up. The play area, dining area, and patio are united by the lawn, which flows around the garden and down onto the patio, hugging the curved wall. The screen of tall plants around the dining area provides shelter as well as protection against stray footballs.

Design considerations

Shape and design

At the initial planning stage it is always best to sketch out a rough outline of how you want the lawn to look and how it will relate to the rest of the garden. Decide whether you want the garden to look formal or informal, if play areas or dining spaces are needed, and consider the practicalities of connecting the different areas together with paths or stepping stones. Be as creative and bold as possible – do not feel that you need be restricted to a rectangular lawn surrounded by narrow flowerbeds. Only when you are completely happy with the design on paper should you begin to physically create the space.

Bordering your lawn

Generally, gardens look bigger and more luxurious when flower borders are wide and generous. Do not be afraid to experiment – alter the depth and shape of the borders to create a striking interaction between lawn and border; sweeping curves can provide a sense of intrigue as flowerbeds lead out of sight and around corners.

Planning access

Creating easy access to important features such as bins, sheds, and compost heaps is important when designing your garden as lawns can be muddy in winter. Paths and stepping stones provide a nice solution to crossing a lawn as they make an attractive feature and can be cheap and easy to install.

Using focal points

Create interest in the garden using focal points such as topiary, statues, bird baths, arches, water features, or sundials. Ornamental trees or even splashes of colourful planting can have the same effect. Focal points draw the eye and help to break up expanses of grass or other plants – use them to unify the garden design.

Assessing your site for a lawn

Before you lay turf or sow any seed it is essential to check some of the key requirements for successful growth, such as soil type, pH, sunlight, and moisture, as these may need adjusting.

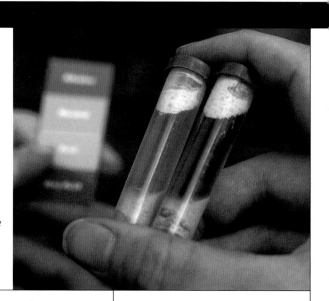

Testing for pH Although most lawn grasses will grow in a range of conditions, the ratio of grasses in your lawn is likely to be dictated by the soil pH, for example rye grasses thrive in slightly alkaline conditions whereas some fescues prefer slightly acidic soil. A pH of 7 is considered neutral; anything higher is alkaline and lower is acidic. Soil testing kits are easy to use and widely available.

Clay soil

This type of soil can be tricky to work with as it is poor-draining. This means that it tends to dry out and become hard in summer but in winter can take on a sticky, muddy texture. However, the advantage of clay is that the soil holds nutrients well and will therefore require minimal feeding. To determine if you have clay soil, roll a small amount into a ball. If the soil sticks together and holds its shape then it is at least partly composed of clay.

Sandy soil

Sandy soils may be easier to dig over than clay due to their relative lightness and crumbly texture, but their major disadvantage is that they aren't able to retain moisture and quickly leach out nutrients. This means that during the summer they will need feeding and the occasional watering to keep grass looking green. Furthermore the soil can shift, leaving hollows and bumps in the lawn – this property also makes them popular with moles.

Improving soils

Most soils will need some sort of improvement to ensure that grass grows as successfully as possible. Adding bulky organic material such as well-rotted manure or compost improves the drainage of clay soil and the structure of sandy soil. This can either be dug or rotavated in to a depth of about 30cm (12in). Lime can be added to slightly acidic soils and sulphur can be used to acidify a soil with high pH.

Aspect

Considering the amount of sun that your garden receives is essential when planning a lawn. Most grass species require a sunny, well-drained site and will struggle in the shade of houses, trees, or fences. The ideal aspect for a lawn is south-facing as this will mean that it receives the maximum amount of sunlight during the day, although it will also mean that it will require the most amount of watering. East-facing lawns will receive the cooler morning sun and west-facing lawns will get the afternoon sun; north-facing lawns will receive the least light. Take photos of your garden throughout the day to help you assess it – for example, the garden shown below faces north-west. Make sure that you select turf or seed mixes that are specially suited for shady and damp sites if necessary.

| Morning | Midday | Evening |

Lie of the land

Slopes have a major effect on growing conditions for a lawn. Generally the conditions will be wetter at the bottom of the slope and drier the further up the slope you go, so you may need to sow more drought-tolerant species at the top of the slope. Gentle slopes can probably be tolerated in most cases, but steep slopes can become slippery and dangerous when wet so it may be worth putting in steps if this is the case (*see right*). It may also be worth terracing a slope into flat sections to create level playing areas for children or areas that can be used for dining and entertaining. Consider drainage too, as the water running off a slope will need to be collected or diverted as it comes down.

Lawn preparation

Careful soil preparation can make the difference between a green healthy lawn and a poor sickly one. Timing is key – start several weeks before you intend to lay turf or sow seed to give the soil enough time to settle.

Seed

Seed is the cheapest method of establishing a lawn and is best sown in early autumn or mid-spring – it will require copious watering if sown in summer. You may need to deter birds by using netting. There are many seed mixes available, including those for shady and damp areas and others that are particularly hard-wearing, so you will easily be able to find a mix to suit your site. Bear in mind that seed can become stale and unusable over time if stored.

Advantages
- The cheapest method of creating a lawn
- There is a good selection of different seed mixes available for difficult sites
- Seed sowing is not as heavy work as lifting turf

Disadvantages
- Grass seed can take a long time to establish
- Some weeds germinate more quickly in the ground than grass seed and will compete with the seedlings for nutrients and light

Turf

Turf is a popular choice as it provides you with an "instant" lawn and can be laid at most times of the year, although extreme periods of cold or hot weather should be avoided. Ideally, turf should be laid almost immediately after it has been delivered but if this isn't feasible, unroll the turves and keep them regularly watered and out of direct sunlight. The soil will need less preparation than for seed sowing as it doesn't have to be reduced to as fine a tilth.

Advantages
- It creates an attractive instant lawn effect
- It can be walked on about a month after laying
- It can be laid in winter when there are fewer gardening jobs to do

Disadvantages
- Turf is a more expensive option than grass seed
- There is less choice in the selection of varieties
- Laying turf can be hard physical work – not advisable for people with bad backs

Preparing the ground

1 Preparation for laying a lawn or sowing grass seed should begin a few weeks before you plan to sow seed or lay turf. Use a fork or spade to dig over the soil to a depth of 30cm (12in). Remove any weeds or stones.

2 Rake the soil level using a large landscape rake. Levelling is important on small lawn areas, but you may want to leave gentle undulations on large, informal sites as natural contours can look attractive.

3 Once the soil has been levelled it should be lightly firmed down to knock out large air pockets and prevent the soil level from dropping too much later. Do this by treading it down with your feet or by using a light roller.

4 Allow the soil to settle for a few weeks before raking it over again, this time using a fine-toothed rake. It will need to be raked to a finer tilth for seed sowing than for laying turf. Remove any weeds that may have appeared.

Sowing grass seed

Sowing grass seed is by far the cheapest method of creating a lawn. The best time to sow seed is in spring or autumn. Seed can be sown in the summer but will need watering regularly; in winter, temperatures are usually too cold for the seed to germinate.

1 Prepare the area to be sown (*see p.29*) and then divide it up into 1m (3ft) squares using canes or string. Measure out the amount of seed required by area as per the supplier's instructions.

2 Sow the measured seed by hand. Half of the seed should be spread in one direction and the other half at 90 degrees to this. Ensure that the seed is distributed as evenly as possible for the best results.

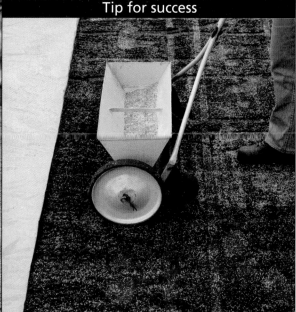

Tip for success

3 Rake the seed in gently. It should ideally be covered by 1–2mm (¹⁄₁₆in) of soil although it can germinate on the surface. Water using a can with a rose or a hose with a spray attachment. Grass will emerge in one to two weeks.

An alternative to hand sowing is to use a seed spreader, which is ideal if you have a large area of ground to cover. It will need to be calibrated to your walking speed so that it distributes seed at the correct rate. Use a sheet to get a neat edge.

Laying turf

The beauty of laying turf is that it produces an instant lawn. It can be laid at most times of the year but will need regular watering during spring and summer. Although it is more expensive than seed, it can be walked on only a few days after laying.

Tip for success

Lay the turf beyond the intended boundaries of the lawn so that it can be trimmed later. Place small pieces of turf away from the edge of the lawn to prevent them from drying out.

1 Prepare the site thoroughly (*see p.29*) and ensure that it is level. Roll the turf out and once in place, firmly tamp down with the back of a rake. If possible, the first row of turf should be laid along a straight edge such as a path.

2 Ensure the ends of each turf are butted up closely to each other and pressed down firmly to prevent them from drying out. The joints of each row should be staggered, a bit like brickwork, as this creates a more sturdy lawn.

3 Stand on a wooden plank so that you do not damage the newly laid turf. Once the lawn is finished, use a stiff broom to brush a good quality top-dressing into any cracks. No top-dressing should be left on the surface.

4 Finally, give the lawn a good watering. Do this frequently over the next few days to draw the roots down into the soil and to help it establish. Once the lawn starts to root it can have its first cut at the mower's maximum height.

Shaping a lawn

Transforming an existing rectangular lawn into a rounded or circular shape can change the whole feel of the garden. It can create extra planting spaces or give new opportunities to use materials such as slate (*shown here*) in the gaps.

1 Take time to measure out the new shape and size of your lawn before beginning the physical work. Sketch out the design on a piece of paper first and then use a tape measure to transfer these measurements onto the lawn.

2 Identify the centre of the circle and place a tent peg in it. Attach a piece of string to it and then holding it taut, swing it around in a circle to the desired size, trailing sand or using spray paint to mark out the circumference.

3 Using the the trail of sand as a guide, firmly cut straight downwards to a depth of about 3–4cm (1¼–1½in) using a half moon cutter. At intervals throughout the process, check that the shape of the circle is even.

4 Slide a spade underneath the turf to be removed and sever the roots away from the soil. Carefully lift the sections of turf and place them upside down in the compost heap to allow them to decompose.

5 Take a strip of strong, flexible edging material and wrap it tightly around the outside of the circle or curve. Push it firmly down into the soil, ensuring that it does not poke up above the surface of the lawn.

6 Add slate, pebbles, or bark chippings to the spaces left by the removed turf, making sure that they sit below the surface of the lawn to make it easier to mow. Alternatively, the gaps could be used as planting pockets.

7 The lawn may need watering around the newly exposed edges until it is established. Use this shaping method for straight-sided shapes as well – use a line of taut string to ensure that you achieve a straight edge.

Assessing your site for a meadow

No garden is too small for a beautiful wildflower meadow so don't be put off if you do not have acres of space. Meadows can be used to great effect sown in pots or flowerbeds and look especially striking mown into sharp shapes on a lawn.

Focal points When creating a wildflower meadow you should consider how it will affect the rest of the garden and how it can be used to enhance other areas. Patches of wildflowers can be focal points in their own right but they can also be used as backdrops or foils to lead the eye to other features such as seating or the white trunk of a silver birch tree.

Shapes, paths, and edging Patches of meadow planting are eye-catching, especially when used to punctuate formal settings; they look particularly striking when cut into sharp shapes or given neat edges, in contrast to their naturally informal look. In a larger garden, a mown path through a wildflower meadow makes a lovely feature, enticing people to walk among the flowers.

Wildlife benefits There are many wild creatures that will benefit from the longer grass and wide range of plants that a wildflower meadow provides. Bees and butterflies will be attracted to the nectar-rich flowers while animals from hedgehogs to harvest mice and swallows will be able to find a home among the diverse plants.

Assessing your site

The ideal site for a meadow is an area of grass, free from vigorous weeds, that can be left to grow long and which has an existing population of native wildflowers that will flower and set seed year after year. Sadly most of us aren't so lucky as to inherit a perfect wildflower meadow and will at the very least have to introduce new plants.

Soil fertility As a rule of thumb wildflower meadows prefer poor, impoverished soil. This is mainly because it prevents coarser grasses such as Yorkshire fog and rye grass competing with and swamping the flowers. If the proposed patch of ground has nettles and docks growing on it then this is a good indication that the ground is nutrient-rich and the fertility needs reducing; similarly if the ground has been enriched over the years with the use of fertilizer and organic matter such as garden compost. One possible option is to remove 10–15cm (4–6in) of topsoil to expose the poorer subsoil underneath. However this is only really practical over a small area of the garden. Another option is to sow yellow rattle (*Rhinanthus minor*) into the existing meadow in early autumn. This semi-parasitic plant attaches to the roots of competing grasses, reducing their vigour.

Drainage Excess moisture can also improve the soil's fertility. If your site is damp, drainage can be improved in small areas by digging sharp sand into the soil. However in large spaces it may be more practical to choose moisture-loving species such as snake's head fritillaries, which will thrive in damp meadow situations.

Perennial weeds It is essential that persistent perennial weeds such as nettles and thistles are removed at the time of sowing or planting as otherwise they may prove difficult to deal with later on.

Impoverishing the soil Over small areas, dig out the top layer of rich topsoil and use it as needed in the rest of the garden so that it doesn't go to waste.

Pick a sunny site Most wildflowers will thrive on a sunny site such as this south-facing slope. Wildflowers make great ground cover on banks that are tricky to mow.

Sowing a meadow

The simplest method of creating a wildflower meadow is to sow seed directly onto the bare soil. It may be necessary to remove the topsoil first as vigorous grasses will compete with the flowers if the soil is too fertile.

1 Check the sowing rates on the labels and measure out the seed required to cover your meadow area. If the seeds are small, mix them with sand so that you will be able to see clearly where they have been spread on the soil surface.

2 Dig over the area and prepare it thoroughly (*see p.29*). Divide out the area to be sown into square metres (three-foot squares) and sow the seeds, spreading half in one direction and the other half in the opposite way.

3 Use a rake to gently bed the seed into the soil – it only needs to be just below the soil surface for successful germination. Birds may target the seed, so cover the seeded area with a net if necessary.

4 With regular watering the wildflower meadow will germinate and produce a stunning display of flowers. It will need cutting down at the end of summer but allow the seeds to fall before removing the material.

Patching with seed

It is not uncommon for existing wildflower meadows to become patchy over time as parts die back and fail to self-seed. If this happens you may wish to sow grass or wildflower seed into the bare patches; this is a useful option if you are covering a large area of ground, as pre-grown plug plants can be relatively expensive.

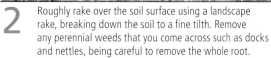

1 In patchy areas that you wish to re-seed, cut down the long grasses using a rotary mower. Begin using the blades on a high setting and then work down until the exposed sections of soil can be seen.

2 Roughly rake over the soil surface using a landscape rake, breaking down the soil to a fine tilth. Remove any perennial weeds that you come across such as docks and nettles, being careful to remove the whole root.

3 Calculate the amount of seed required, measure it out, and then distribute it over the bare patches. Gently rake it into the ground using a fine rake. Continue this process for other bare patches in the meadow.

4 Annual seeds flower after a few weeks; perennials, such as *Verbena bonariensis*, shown, may not flower in their first year. Cut the plants back once the flowers have died. Rake up the clippings to ensure the soil fertility stays low.

Using ground cover

Ground-cover plants are useful for filling awkward spaces that might otherwise be left as bare soil or covered over with hard landscaping. Choose ground cover for its foliage, flowers, or scent to make the most of every available surface.

Filling gaps Many ground-cover plants can be used to add interest and colour to the spaces between patio slabs or steps where weeds may otherwise grow. Many of these plants are tough enough to withstand some light footfall, such as chamomile and thyme.

On a bank There can be many spaces in a garden where mowing is difficult or even impossible due to the angle of the terrain, such as a bank or steep slope. Ground-cover plants are ideal for use in these spaces where good coverage but minimal maintenance is needed.

Underneath trees Many lawn grasses will struggle to grow successfully in the shady areas created by the foliage of trees. However, there are many attractive, shade-loving ground-cover plants such as ferns and ivies that will thrive in these locations.

Sedum roof Despite being classed as "ground cover", many plants are also useful when grown in other locations, such as the sedums on this stunning roof. They will grow successfully in less than favourable, dry, and exposed conditions where many other plants would fail.

Planning and planting

Choose ground-cover plants that will thrive in your conditions – for example, some plants, such as *Genista* or *Nepeta,* will thrive in hot, dry sites, whereas hellebores, hostas, and *Sarcococca* prefer damp shade (*see pp.130– 137*). Some plants can survive impoverished, compacted soil but most will benefit from some soil preparation before planting. Dig over the ground thoroughly and remove any weeds. Incorporate plenty of organic material such as garden compost and then rake the soil level. Check planting distances carefully on the plant labels and space out accordingly before planting (*see right*). Be aware that some plants may look small in the pot but once planted out can be extremely vigorous and invasive. One of the benefits of planting ground cover is that it can help to smother weeds, although while plants are young and small they won't be very effective. To reduce the need for weeding, lay black landscape fabric first and then plant through slits made with a gardening knife. Bear in mind however that if the plants spread or creep by laying down roots, for example ivies, then this will prevent them from becoming effective ground cover.

General planting tips

Digging in grit Heavy soils such as clay will benefit from the addition of about a bucketful of horticultural grit per square metre (yard) of soil to improve its drainage.

Planting Most ground-cover plants, particularly shrubs, benefit from having their roots teased out prior to planting to ensure that they grow outwards rather than circling inwards.

Layering Plants such as ivy spread by sending out roots when their stems come into contact with the soil. Assist this development by lightly pegging sections of stem into the soil.

Embellishing your lawn

For many people the lawn is the most prominent feature of the garden, so make sure yours looks as attractive as possible by trying a few simple but effective embellishments. The step-by-step guides in this chapter will show you how to set your lawn apart: add attractive edging in a range of materials; construct a brick mowing strip to make cutting the grass easy; add splashes of colour by naturalizing spring- or autumn-flowering bulbs; add height and interest by planting an ornamental tree as a focal point; and plant chamomile as an attractive scented alternative to grass. In addition, if you find the chore of cutting the grass too much, this chapter also includes a step-by-step guide to laying artificial turf.

Choosing and using edging materials

It isn't essential to use edging around a lawn, but it does create a neater, more distinctive feature of the grass and reduces the chore of keeping the edges tidy.

Tip for success

Wooden edging should be painted or treated with a wood preservative to prevent it rotting. Do this 24 hours prior to inserting the edging panels into the ground.

| 1 | Peg a line of string taut along the desired edge and use a half moon cutter to create a groove in the turf to a depth of about 7cm (3in). Remove any excess turf and push back some of the soil so it will be easier to insert the edging. | 2 | Place the sections of wooden edging over the groove and lightly tap them down using a hammer or rubber mallet. Place a piece of wood between the hammer and the edging to avoid damaging it. |

Alternatives

Wide brick edge Laid flat, bricks give a smart finish to a lawn and are suitable for both formal and informal areas. If they are laid beneath the level of the turf then they make an ideal mowing edge (*see pp.46–47*).

Brick diamonds For an attractive rustic effect, bricks can be laid on their sides around the edge of the lawn. They should be laid diagonally with about half of the brick in the soil and the remainder above ground.

Victorian-style stone Giving a sense of formality to a lawn, this style of edging looks good in the gardens of Victorian town houses where it will complement the architecture. This style is also popular in terracotta.

Install a mowing strip of bricks

Ideally, lawns shouldn't be laid directly up to walls or fences as this can make mowing difficult and you may find you need to use a strimmer to tidy the edges. To avoid this, lay a line of bricks alongside the lawn.

Tip for success

For a curved lawn edge, mark out the mowing strip using a hosepipe or a line of sand. Position the bricks following the inner curve; the space between the bricks will be greater at the mowing strip's outer edge.

1 Use a brick to establish the width of the mowing strip required and then mark it out using string and pegs. Use a half moon cutter or a spade to cut down along the line to the depth of the brick.

2 Use a spade or turfing iron to cut along the bottom of the turf, keeping the tool as level as possible. The turf can either be re-laid in the garden or stacked upside down and left to decompose into compost.

3 Create a wet mortar mix of three parts sand to one part cement and place a thin layer of it in the bottom of the trench. Lay the bricks on top and use a rubber mallet to tap them down, ensuring that they are level.

4 Finally, use a dry mix of mortar using the same ratio of sand to cement, and brush it between the gaps in the bricks, using a trowel or brush. Wet the mortar by sprinkling water over the bricks using a watering can.

Laying stepping stones

A simple feature to design and create, stepping stones can look very attractive in a lawn. They help to prevent the wear and tear of frequently walked areas of ground and they will also prevent your shoes getting muddy in winter.

Tip for success

Ensure that you lay your stepping stones about 5mm (¼in) below the surface of the lawn so that the grass can be cut without damaging the blades of the lawnmower.

1 By measuring the length of your stride, calculate how many stepping stones will be needed. Lay them in place on the lawn and double check the spacing. Once you are satisfied, cut around them using a sharp garden knife.

2 Lift the slab and remove the square of grass, using a spade to cut underneath the turf. Using a trowel, dig out some of the excess soil so that the hole is about 2.5cm (1in) deeper than the depth of the paving slab.

3 Using a trowel, place a 1cm (½in) layer of soft sand into the bottom of the hole, level it out, and then compact it. This helps to ensure that the area won't sink once the paving slabs have been placed in position.

4 Mix up cement and sand at a ratio of 1:4. Gradually add water until the mortar is thick but workable and then lay this in the bottom of the hole. Set the slab on top, ensuring it is level and sitting just below the surface of the lawn.

Patch planting meadow flowers

Planting small plugs of wildflowers in an existing lawn is an easy way to establish an attractive meadow. Plants can be grown from seed and then planted out, but a wide range of plug plants is available from garden centres.

1 Cut the grass short prior to planting and rake up and remove the clippings. Randomly distribute the plug plants across the lawn area so that the planting will look natural. Avoid planting in rows or patterns that look symmetrical.

2 Using a trowel, dig holes where the plug plants have been placed and slot them into the ground. Firm the plants in using your fingers. You may wish to use a bulb planter if you are planting over a large area.

3 Repeat this process until you have achieved an even spread of plants across the meadow area. Once all the plants are in place they should be well watered. Avoid walking on areas that have been recently planted.

4 Do not apply fertilizers to the lawn as this will encourage the grasses to compete with the meadow flowers. Avoid cutting the grass until the plants have finished flowering so that they have a chance to disperse their seed.

Alternative plants

A wide range of plants can be used to create a wildflower meadow. Other than the examples given here, plants to try include grasses such as *Cynosurus cristatus* (crested dog's tail), *Deschampsia cespitosa* (tufted hair grass), and *Agrostis capillaris* (common bent). Bulbs such as bluebells, grape hyacinths, and crocuses in spring, camassias in summer, and colchicums in autumn will give attractive year-round colour.

Pilosella aurantiaca
(fox and cubs)

Knautia arvensis
(field scabious)

Geranium pratense
(meadow cranesbill)

Primula veris
(cowslip)

Silene dioica
(red campion)

Leucanthemum vulgare
(ox-eye daisy)

Prunella vulgaris
(self heal)

Achillea millefolium
(yarrow)

Planting trees in a lawn

Trees add height and colour to a garden and look stunning planted in a beautifully mown lawn and underplanted with bulbs. Choose trees that provide more than one period of interest in the year such as blossom in spring, berries in late summer, foliage with autumn colour, and attractive bark for winter.

1 Give the tree a good watering prior to planting. Those in containers are available to buy all year round, but some trees can be bought "bare root" and should be planted during autumn and winter.

2 Dig out a hole at least twice the circumference of the tree's container but no deeper than the depth of the root ball. Don't loosen the soil in the bottom of the hole however, as this could cause the tree to sink after planting.

3 Place the tree into the hole and use a garden cane to ensure that the top of the root ball is level with the surrounding ground. Adjust the depth accordingly; if the hole is too deep, replace some of the soil.

Planting trees in a lawn *continued*

4 Mix the excavated soil with well-rotted manure. Remove the tree from its container and gently tease the outer roots out. Water the hole well and then place the tree back into it. Gradually replace the soil, watering as you go.

5 Drive a wooden stake into the ground next to the tree at an angle of 45 degrees. Position it on the side of the tree that faces the prevailing wind, ensuring that it doesn't damage the roots. Attach it using a tree tie.

6 Use well-rotted manure or a good quality garden compost to mulch around the base of the tree; this helps to suppress weeds and to retain moisture. Keep the mulch away from the trunk to prevent it rotting.

7 Give the tree a good soaking with water. Young trees will need watering almost every day for their first few months, especially during spring and summer, until they are fully established in the ground.

Staking options

Two-stake method This technique is useful for top-heavy trees or for standards, which can be prone to snap below the head if placed in exposed or windy places. Using elastic tree ties allows the tree to flex while supporting it enough to prevent it blowing over.

Upright stake Vertical stakes can only be used on bare-root trees as it isn't possible to get the stake close enough to the tree on container-grown types because these have larger root balls. Insert the stake prior to planting to avoid damaging the root system.

Guy ropes Established trees that have been moved to a new site benefit from a system of wires attached high up on the trunk. This offers good support but requires a large space. Take care as the wires can be a trip hazard.

Naturalizing bulbs in grass

When naturalized, bulbs create a spectacular splash of colour on the lawn. Most bulbs, including daffodils and bluebells, bloom in the springtime but with careful planning you can grow flowers in the lawn all year round.

1 To make the planting look natural, scatter the bulbs across the lawn and plant them where they land. Use a bulb planter to take out a core of soil; bulbs should be planted at two to three times their depth.

2 Place the bulb in the bottom of the hole with its growing tip facing upwards. If the soil is poorly drained, grit or sand can be added. After planting, backfill the hole with soil and replace the plug of turf.

3 After the plant has flowered it should be deadheaded and left for a few weeks until the foliage has died back, allowing nutrients to return to the bulb. Then mow the faded foliage and give the lawn a light rolling to level it.

An alternative method of planting bulbs is to peel back the turf and plant them in clusters. This is a useful and quick technique to use if there are a lot of bulbs to plant, or if they are small and need to be planted close together.

1 Use a half moon cutter or a spade to cut an "H" shape and then slice under the turf horizontally. Carefully peel the flaps of turf back. Lightly loosen the soil in the hole and add grit or sand if the soil is badly drained.

2 Scatter the bulbs on the earth, ensuring that their placement looks natural. Plant them at the required depth, which is usually two to three times their height, with their growing tips facing upwards.

3 Once the bulbs are planted, roll the turf back into place ensuring that they are completely covered. Firm the turf down well with the back of a rake, checking that the area is level with the rest of the lawn. Water in well.

4 When the bulbs are in flower, take care when mowing the lawn around them. Patches of flowering bulbs nestled in unmown grass look attractive when surrounded with a contrasting, neatly mown lawn.

Planting snowdrops under a tree

The delicate, nodding white heads of snowdrops are a heart-warming sight; their flowering is one of the first signs that spring is on its way. Suitable for shady, moist, well-drained sites, they are ideal for planting in clumps under trees.

1 The best time to buy or to lift and divide snowdrops is when they are "in the green" – when they are in full leaf, either in flower or just after. Use a trowel or hand fork to dig them up, taking care not to damage the bulbs.

2 Gently prise the clumps of bulbs apart with your hands. If the plant is still in flower, the blooms should be picked off to help conserve the energy of the plant. Divide large clumps into clusters of about three or four bulbs.

3 Dig a hole using a trowel or spade to about 10–15cm (4–6in) deep, ideally under the canopy of the tree or in light shade. On heavy or badly drained soil it may be necessary to add horticultural grit or sharp sand.

4 Plant out, ensuring that most of the leaf is above ground. Fill around the bulbs with soil and gently firm in. Water the plants in well. Leave them to die back in their first year; in later years, mow after the leaves have died back.

Planting a chamomile lawn

Chamomile is a low-growing, creeping perennial that creates a rich tapestry of deep green foliage when closely planted. It releases a delicate aroma when walked on. These lawns are easy to create and their fast-growing habit means that they establish quickly.

Tip for success

Any variety of chamomile can be used in a lawn but the best is non-flowering 'Treneague'. However, chamomile lawns are not as resilient as grass and should only be walked on occasionally.

1 Prepare the ground thoroughly, adding horticultural grit or sharp sand if it is heavy or badly drained, and ensure that all weeds are cleared. Divide the chamomile plants into segments ensuring that each part has plenty of root.

2 Chamomile has a fast-growing, creeping habit, so ensure that the plants have space to spread. Lay them out, positioning them about 8–15cm (4–6in) apart. Plant the chamomile and then firm in well with your fingertips.

Alternative plants

3 After planting, give the chamomile a good watering. Regularly water the plants throughout the summer months to prevent them from drying out. Do not walk on the lawn for about three months to give it time to establish.

Thyme is a useful alternative to chamomile and has a similar low-growing habit with aromatic foliage, which releases a wonderful scent when walked on. Its attractive pink flowers are popular with bees and butterflies. The plants need light pruning in late summer.

Laying artificial turf

It may not be for everyone, but artificial grass has seen a rise in popularity in recent years – with its easy upkeep and year-round vibrancy it's easy to see why. It is available in a range of textures and shades and can be fitted to any design.

Tip for success

If you are covering a large area and need to butt two widths together, apply a thin layer of adhesive on the surface beneath the joint to stop the two pieces shifting or buckling.

1 Remove any existing turf using a spade or turf cutter and then dig the soil out to a depth of approximately 4–6cm (1½–2½in). The artificial grass will need to sit approximately 15mm (½in) above any edging.

2 In order to prevent weeds from growing up through the turf and causing it to buckle or disfigure, lay a sheet of weed-suppressing membrane over your lawn space and cut it to shape using a stanley knife.

3 Apply a thin aggregate layer of sand, crushed stones, or grit over the membrane, and compact it to create a solid base. This layer will provide you with a firm, well-draining surface that will support the rest of the materials.

4 Once the layer of aggregate is in place, apply a 1–2cm (½–¾in) layer of sharp sand, to give an even surface. Compact the sand and level it, smoothing the surface using a piece of wood or a screed bar with a level.

Laying artificial turf *continued*

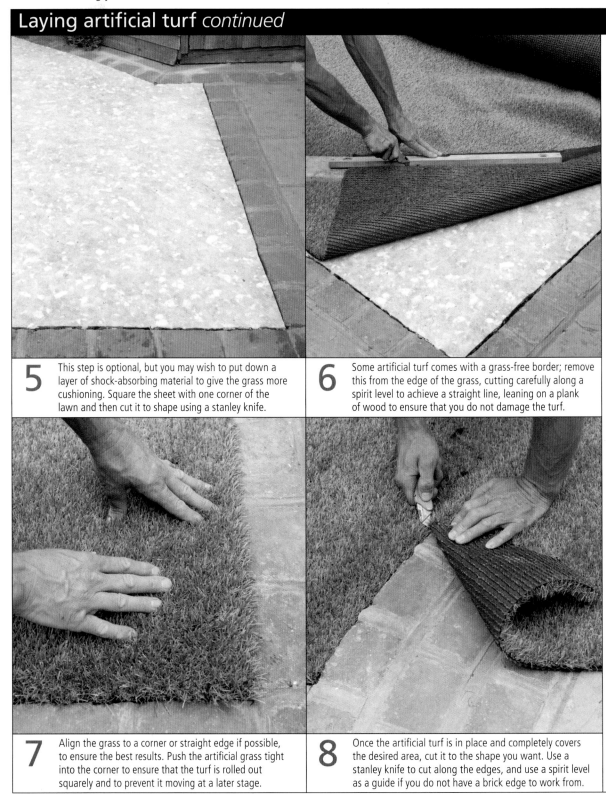

5 This step is optional, but you may wish to put down a layer of shock-absorbing material to give the grass more cushioning. Square the sheet with one corner of the lawn and then cut it to shape using a stanley knife.

6 Some artificial turf comes with a grass-free border; remove this from the edge of the grass, cutting carefully along a spirit level to achieve a straight line, leaning on a plank of wood to ensure that you do not damage the turf.

7 Align the grass to a corner or straight edge if possible, to ensure the best results. Push the artificial grass tight into the corner to ensure that the turf is rolled out squarely and to prevent it moving at a later stage.

8 Once the artificial turf is in place and completely covers the desired area, cut it to the shape you want. Use a stanley knife to cut along the edges, and use a spirit level as a guide if you do not have a brick edge to work from.

9 Once you are happy that the grass is the correct shape and size, nail it in place. Start by securing each corner and then insert nails every 30–40cm (12–16in) along each edge. Use adhesive if you are covering a vertical surface.

10 Using a spreader to ensure even coverage, apply a thin layer of silica sand directly to the lawn surface. This will help to provide a stabilizing effect on the artificial grass and will help to prevent it moving.

11 Brush the silica sand into the grass surface using a coarse broom. The grass will require little upkeep, although if the blades become flattened, lift them by brushing over with a broom. If necessary, wash with warm, soapy water.

Planting recipes

Create stunning planting combinations by following these simple recipes in your garden. The easy-to-achieve designs can transform an outside space and can be adapted to suit any garden size or planting style. The symbols below are used to indicate the conditions that the plants prefer.

Key to plant symbols

ᵧ   Plants given the RHS Award of Garden Merit

Soil preference

◊   Well-drained soil

◊   Moist soil

●   Wet soil

Preference for sun or shade

☼   Full sun

☼   Partial or dappled shade

☀   Full shade

Hardiness ratings

✳✳✳   Fully hardy plants

✳✳   Plants that survive outside in mild regions or sheltered sites

✳   Plants that need protection from frost over winter

Feathery foliage

This recipe uses ornamental grasses to form a stunning composition of colourful, fluffy seedheads, and architectural foliage and is easily achieved in the smallest of sunny borders. The tall *Stipa* and *Miscanthus* grasses add upright structure at the back of the design while the beautiful pinkish seedheads of *Pennisetum alopecuroides* provide the eye-catching focus in the centre. The contrasting colours of the blue *Elymus* and the golden *Hakonechloa* bring a range of colour to the design.

Grass basics

Size 3x1.5m (10x5ft)
Suits Contemporary gardens
Soil Free-draining
Site Full sun to partial shade

Shopping list

- 2 x *Stipa calamagrostis*
- 1 x *Miscanthus sinensis* 'Zebrinus'
- 1 x *Miscanthus sinensis* 'Morning Light'
- 2 x *Pennisetum alopecuroides*
- 3 x *Hakonechloa macra* 'Aureola'
- 1 x *Elymus magellanicus*

Planting and aftercare

Dig over the soil and rake it level. Lay down landscape fabric to prevent weeds from germinating and cut slits where the plants are to be slotted. The *Stipa calamagrostis* and the *Miscanthus sinensis* 'Zebrinus' are the tallest plants so position these towards the back, 50cm (20in) apart. Place the others in the foreground, about 20cm (8in) apart. Cover any visible landscape fabric with gravel. Water regularly in the first year until the grasses are established. They are deciduous but can be left over winter to provide structure and wildlife interest and should then be cut back in February. This design is relatively low maintenance as grasses require no deadheading, pruning, or staking, while the landscape fabric will help to smother weeds.

Stipa calamagrostis
✿✿✿ ◊ ☀

Miscanthus sinensis 'Zebrinus'
✿✿✿ ◊ ☀ ♈

Miscanthus sinensis 'Morning Light'
✿✿✿ ◊ ☀ ♈

Pennisetum alopecuroides
✿✿✿ ◊ ☀

Hakonechloa macra 'Aureola'
✿✿✿ ◑ ☀ ♈

Elymus magellanicus
✿✿✿ ◊ ☀

Spring medley

Naturalistic plantings of bulbs in grass can bring a plain expanse of lawn to life, and look especially striking when planted under trees. The delicate, nodding white heads of snowdrops (*Galanthus* 'S. Arnott') and vibrantly coloured crocuses ('Pickwick' and 'Yellow Giant') break up the sea of grass and create an attractive focal point. In this design, the bulbs have been planted in groups so that their bold blocks of colour create maximum impact. The planting scheme has a natural feel, with the different groups allowed to drift into each other.

Bulb basics

Size 10x10m (30x30ft)
Suits Lawn areas, under trees, wildlife gardens, meadows
Soil Free-draining or slightly moist soil
Site Full sun to partial shade

Shopping list

- 500 bulbs x *Crocus* 'Yellow Giant'
- 500 bulbs x *Crocus vernus* 'Pickwick'
- 200 bulbs x *Galanthus* 'S. Arnott'

Planting and aftercare

Crocus bulbs should be planted in autumn. Scatter the bulbs randomly on the ground to make the planting look natural and plant them where they fall. Use a bulb planter to put them in the ground or in larger spaces, use a turf cutter to lift up large sections of turf before planting the bulbs and replacing the grass (*see pp.56–57*). The bulbs should be planted at about two times the depth of their height; ensure that the bulbs are planted the right way up. Transplant young snowdrop plants in late spring, while they are "in the green" (*see pp.58–59*). Allow the foliage of the bulbs to die back after flowering as this allows nutrients to return to the bulb ensuring a good show of flowers the following year. They can then be cut back with a rotary mower.

Crocus 'Yellow Giant'
❀❀❀ ◊ ◊ ☼

Crocus vernus 'Pickwick'
❀❀❀ ◊ ◊ ☼

Galanthus 'S. Arnott'
❀❀❀ ◊ ◊ ☼ ☼ ♈

Alternative plant idea

Scilla siberica 'Spring Beauty'
❀❀❀ ◊ ◊ ☼ ☼

A splash of colour

This rainbow palette of wildflowers ranges from fiery reds to vibrant purples and should give a dazzling display of colour from late spring through to the end of summer. The beauty of this recipe is that it will grow in a few weeks and all it costs is the price of a few packets of seeds. All the plants here are annuals except for ox-eye daisy (*Leucanthemum vulgare*), which is a perennial and will establish better if bought as a plug plant.

Meadow basics

Size 4x3m (12x10ft)
Suits Sunny borders, informal gardens
Soil Free-draining or slightly moist soil
Site Full sun

Shopping list

- 30 plug plants x *Leucanthemum vulgare* (ox-eye daisy)
- 2 packets of seed x *Papaver rhoeas* (annual poppy)
- 2 packets of seed x *Agrostemma githago* (corncockle)
- 2 packets of seed x *Centaurea cyanus* (cornflower)
- 2 packets of seed x *Glebionis segetum* (corn marigold)

Planting and aftercare

In early spring, clear any plants or weeds from the site, dig over the soil and rake it level. It is important to get an even spread of flowers so mix up all the seed in a bucket and add sand to it to make distribution easier. Sow the seed evenly and then gently rake it in (*see p.38*). Plant the ox-eye daisy plug plants in among the seed. Water the plants in well and keep them well watered during the first few weeks. After flowering, allow the seedheads to ripen before either shaking them onto the soil for the following year or collecting them in paper bags, to be sown later. Remove all the plants except for the ox-eye daisies and add them to the compost heap.

Leucanthemum vulgare
❀❀❀ ○ ☼

Papaver rhoeas
❀❀❀ ○ ☼

Agrostemma githago
❀❀❀ ○ ☼

Centaurea cyanus
❀❀❀ ○ ☼

Glebionis segetum
❀❀❀ ○ ☼

Alternative plant idea

Anthemis punctata
❀❀❀ ○ ☼

Prairie-style planting

The abundance of soft, textural plants in fiery, contrasting colours makes prairie-style planting very attractive and rightly popular. The planting is informal in style with no need for staking – plant drifts of flowers that overlap and blend into one another. All the plants in this recipe are very attractive to bees and butterflies as they provide a rich source of nectar.

Prairie basics

Size 3x3m (10x10ft)
Suits Informal planting schemes, gravel gardens, herbaceous borders, meadows
Soil Free-draining
Site Full sun

Shopping list

- 5 x *Echinacea pallida*
- 5 x *Echinacea paradoxa*
- 5 x *Asclepias tuberosa*
- 5 x *Dianthus carthusianorum*

Planting and aftercare

Dig over the ground, adding organic matter to very sandy soils, and rake level. Plant in loose drifts or clusters, spacing the plants about 45cm (18in) apart, but allowing the different groups to blend into each other slightly for a natural look. Give the plants a good watering and add a layer of gravel mulch around them to help suppress weeds. Although the plants are herbaceous it is worth waiting until early spring to cut them back as they will provide seedheads for wildlife and an attractive winter structure. The plants are relatively low maintenance and shouldn't require deadheading. However, it might be worth cutting back the new growth of some of the plants in May (which is known as the Chelsea chop) as this will help to extend the flowering season and will create an interesting variety of heights within the design. All the plants in this recipe are perennials and will benefit from being divided every few years in spring.

Echinacea pallida
❀❀❀ ◊ ☼

Echinacea paradoxa
❀❀❀ ◊ ☼

Asclepias tuberosa
❀❀❀ ◊ ☼

Dianthus carthusianorum
❀❀❀ ◊ ☼

Woodland wonderland

This woodland planting gives a sense of calm serenity. The soft colours of the geraniums and foxgloves (*Digitalis purpurea*) mingle with the dark orange flower bracts of the *Euphorbia* and are striking against a sea of deep green foliage. These plants are ideal for a woodland situation as they can cope with the light shade and shortage of moisture that are caused by the canopies and roots of the trees.

Woodland basics

Size 3x3m (10x10ft)
Suits Woodland gardens, shady herbaceous borders
Soil Free-draining
Site Dappled shade

Shopping list

- 3 x *Digitalis purpurea* (foxglove)
- 7 x *Geranium* Patricia ('Brempat')
- 1 x *Euphorbia griffithii* 'Dixter'

Planting and aftercare

Lightly dig over the soil being careful not to damage any tree roots. Incorporate plenty of organic matter such as leafmould or compost into the planting area and then rake it level. Plant the geraniums in the centre of the space, about 60cm (24in) apart, as they can spread rapidly. The *Euphorbia* can be planted in the foreground and if you choose to plant any *Epimedium*, these should be positioned around the outside of the planting scheme to form a "foliage frame". The foxgloves should be dotted about among the geraniums towards the back of the design, to give it some height. The plants should be watered in well. The geraniums and *Euphorbia* can be cut back after flowering as they are perennial. As the foxglove is a biennial it should be left to drop its seeds. Be careful not to get the milky sap of the *Euphorbia* on the skin as it can be an irritant and may burn.

Digitalis purpurea
✿✿✿ ◊ ◑ ☼ ☀

Geranium Patricia ('Brempat')
✿✿✿ ◊ ☼ ☀ ♈

Euphorbia griffithii 'Dixter'
✿✿✿ ◊ ☼ ☀ ♈

Alternative plant idea

Epimedium x perralchicum 'Wisley'
✿✿✿ ◊ ◑ ☀

Rooftop gardening

Living roofs are increasing in popularity for a number of reasons: they can be grown in even tiny gardens, they bring colour to bare, unused outdoor surfaces, they insulate your roof, and they can provide extra wildlife habitats. This simple recipe uses just three cultivars of sedum to create a rich tapestry of red and gold. Sedums are ideal roof plants as they are drought tolerant and will cover the surface by forming a thick mat of succulent foliage.

Sedum basics

Size 1.5x2.5m (5x8ft)
Suits Strong garden roofs
Soil Free-draining
Site Full sun

Shopping list

- 10 x *Sedum tetractinum* 'Coral Reef'
- 10 x *Sedum rupestre* 'Angelina'
- 10 x *Sedum selskianum* 'Spirit'

Planting and aftercare

Cut a piece of marine-quality plywood to the size of the roof and cover it with butyl liner. Nail this securely to the roof. Create a 5cm (2in) deep wooden planting frame on top by fastening planks of wood to each edge of the roof to form a sturdy framework. Fill the frame with a mix of perlite, rockwool, and general compost. Drill holes into the wooden frame's bottom edge to promote good drainage. Push rockwool into these holes as a filter to prevent the compost from draining out too. Plant the sedums into the growing medium. Sedums don't like wet roots so in autumn or winter clear the leaves that will have fallen on the plants and check that the drainage holes are still open. Alternatively, purpose-made sedum roof mats can be bought that can simply be rolled out and attached. If you are unsure whether your roof can take the weight of the sedum planting scheme, check with a surveyor.

Sedum tetractinum 'Coral Reef'
❀❀❀ ◊ ☼

Sedum rupestre 'Angelina'
❀❀❀ ◊ ☼

Sedum selskianum 'Spirit'
❀❀❀ ◊ ☼

Alternative plant idea

Sedum spurium 'Schorbuser Blut'
❀❀❀ ◊ ☼ ♈

Ground cover for sun

This shimmering silver design is ideal for sites that receive a lot of sunshine. The dominant ground-cover plant is *Artemisia schmidtiana* 'Nana', which runs through the design like a river, pooling around the taller structural plants at the rear. In the foreground the ornamental blue grasses create a textural contrast with their long, spiky blades of foliage. Ornamental pink thrift (*Armeria maritima* 'Splendens'), flowers from spring until early summer and adds a splash of colour.

Ground cover basics

Size 1.8x1.5m (6x5ft)
Suits Warm, sheltered gardens
Soil Sharply drained
Site Full sun

Shopping list

- 7 x *Festuca glauca* 'Blauglut'
- 3 x *Artemisia ludoviciana* 'Valerie Finnis'
- 7 x *Artemisia schmidtiana* 'Nana'
- 3 x *Astelia chathamica*
- 9 x *Armeria maritima* 'Splendens'

Planting and aftercare

These plants are typical of Mediterranean planting schemes and thrive in dry, arid conditions. Add horticultural grit to the soil if it is heavy and cut back surrounding shrubs and tree branches if they block out any sunlight. Plant the tall *Astelia* and cut-leaved *Artemisia* at the back to give the recipe some height, positioning the colourful *Armeria* in front. Plant the *Artemisia* 'Nana' in a zigzag pattern across the centre of the bed and finally the grasses in the foreground. Plant in spring so that the slightly tender *Astelia* have a chance to establish before the onset of winter. This recipe is relatively low maintenance: cut back the dead stems of the pink thrift after flowering. The *Astelia* may need covering with horticultural fleece in cooler areas during winter and you may need to remove some of the dead grass foliage in spring.

Festuca glauca 'Blauglut'
❀❀❀ ◊ ☼

Artemisia ludoviciana 'Valerie Finnis'
❀❀ ◊ ☼ ♈

Artemisia schmidtiana 'Nana'
❀❀❀ ◊ ☼ ♈

Astelia chathamica
❀❀ ◊ ◐ ☼ ◑ ♈

Armeria maritima 'Splendens'
❀❀❀ ◊ ☼

Ground cover for shade

This lush, natural-looking planting recipe, shown here in a dappled glade of silver birches, can be easily recreated in any shady area of the garden, whether or not you have trees. The limited colour palette gives a tranquil, calming feel: the golden foliage of *Carex elata* 'Aurea' complements the soft greens and whites of *Dryopteris filix-mas* and *Aquilegia vulgaris* var. *stellata* 'Greenapples', making the vibrant purple flowers of *Polemonium yezoense* var. *hidakanum* 'Purple Rain' all the more striking.

Ground cover basics

Size 3x3m (10x10ft)
Suits Shady patio, courtyard, or terrace, light woodland
Soil Free-draining
Site Dappled shade

Shopping list

- 5 x *Carex elata* 'Aurea'
- 5 x *Dryopteris filix-mas*
- 5 x *Aquilegia vulgaris* var. *stellata* 'Greenapples'
- 2 x *Polemonium yezoense* var. *hidakanum* 'Purple Rain'
- 7 x *Epimedium* x *perralchicum* 'Fröhnleiten'

Planting and aftercare

Lightly dig over the soil before planting, being careful not to damage any tree roots. The plants should be positioned as randomly as possible – lay them out while they are still in their pots to make sure you get an even, natural-looking spread. Dot the *Dryopteris* and *Carex* about, allowing about 30cm (12in) between plants, and then position the nodding *Aquilegia* and scrambling *Epimedium* between them to fill in the gaps. These plants will require little maintenance but it is important that the growth of the *Epimedium* is kept in check so that it doesn't swamp any of the other less vigorous plants.

Carex elata 'Aurea'
❁❁❁ ◊ ◖ ☼ ☀ ⚲

Dryopteris filix-mas
❁❁❁ ◖ ☼ ⚲

Polemonium yezoense var. *hidakanum* 'Purple Rain' ❁❁❁ ◊ ◖ ☼ ☀

Aquilegia vulgaris var. *stellata* 'Greenapples' ❁❁❁ ◊ ☼ ☀

Epimedium x *perralchicum* 'Fröhnleiten' ❁❁❁ ◊ ◖ ☼ ☀ ⚲

Caring for your lawn

To keep your lawn looking its best it will need regular maintenance in the form of watering, feeding, weeding, and top-dressing, and may even need the occasional specialist repair. To help you provide the best possible care, this chapter contains a guide to help you choose the right lawn tool for the job as well as giving you information on the best mowing techniques. The Seasonal Planner will help you stay ahead of the game by telling you at what time of year specific jobs should be done. The following pages will also help you to identify the main weeds, pests, and diseases that can afflict your lawn and, most importantly, how to deal with them.

Seasonal planner: spring and summer

This planner outlines the different lawn care tasks that should be performed throughout the year.

Follow these simple seasonal guidelines to make sure that your lawn looks healthy and green all year round.

Spring

Spring is the season when a lawn really needs some tender loving care as temperatures rise and the grass starts to grow, increasing its reliance on water and fertilizer.

Laying turf and sowing seed
Early spring is a good time for turf laying as the risk of frost is reduced, making the soil more workable. Spring is also the ideal time for sowing seed as the soil warms up and there is usually enough rain to encourage germination.

Feeding
A spring feed is essential to keep the lawn looking green. There are many pre-packaged feeds available – the main ingredient is nitrogen, which encourages strong growth.

Watering
Towards the end of spring it may be necessary to water occasionally if the last few months have been dry.

Mowing
Cut the grass regularly ensuring that the mower is raised to its highest setting for the first few cuts.

Scarifying
Lightly scarify the lawn using a spring-tined rake or a mechanical scarifier to remove dead grass (thatch).

Aerating
Use a fork or aerator to spike the lawn: this allows air to circulate at the grass roots and breaks up compacted soil.

Summer

Summer is the period when grass is at its most stressed, which means that some operations such as scarifying or aerating should be avoided in periods of drought.

Feeding
If necessary, lawns can receive another feed of fertilizer during the summer, but only if rainfall is predicted. In extremely dry or hot weather fertilizer will scorch and stress the lawn. As an alternative to granular fertilizer, liquid feeds such as seaweed tonics can be applied.

Watering
To keep the lawn green during a dry summer it may be necessary to water it with an irrigation system, or manually with a hosepipe. However, lawns can recover quickly from drought and as water conservation is important, try to avoid watering except in extreme conditions.

Mowing
Lawns will need mowing once or twice a week although this should be stopped during extremely dry periods.

Weeding
Continue to remove pernicious weeds such as dandelions by digging them out of the ground, taking care to remove the whole root. Others such as speedwell, clovers, and daisies usually need spraying to remove them properly – this should be avoided during periods of drought.

Spring is the ideal time to lay turf as the weather warms up and showers reduce the need for watering.

Mowing becomes a regular job in summer but it should be avoided in extremely dry conditions.

Seasonal planner: autumn and winter

Autumn

This is the key season for lawn renovations. Autumn care will help to ensure that the lawn survives the low temperatures of winter. It will also help the lawn to recover from its heavy usage during spring and summer.

Feeding

Whereas spring feeds are high in nitrogen to encourage the lawn to grow, the key ingredient in autumn feeds is potassium as this encourages strong growth and will toughen up the grass for winter.

Top-dressing

Spread a good quality top-dressing evenly over the lawn and then brush into the holes created by aerating; ensure that it is all brushed in otherwise it will kill the grass. Proprietary mixes can be bought, but you can make your own by mixing sand, good quality compost, and loam.

Mowing

Lawns will still need an occasional cut on a high setting. The last cut of the year should be in late autumn.

Scarifying

Use a spring-tined rake or a mechanical scarifier to rip the thatch out of the lawn. Scarify in two directions, the second time deeper than the first; this scarification should be more vigorous than the spring scarification. Rake up all the removed thatch and add it to the compost heap.

Aerating

The lawn should be spiked down to about 8–10cm (3–4in) with either a fork or a mechanical aerator. Solid tining should be done every year, and about every three or four years hollow tining can be carried out instead (see p.95).

Renovating turf

This is a good time to lay turf or seed the lawn as the soil will be warm. This should also allow enough time for the lawn to establish itself before the onset of winter. Patches can be re-turfed and hollows and bumps smoothed out. Sow grass seed on bare patches of lawn.

Winter

There is little to do with the lawn during winter; avoid walking on it during frosty periods as this can leave black marks where the grass will eventually die back.

Laying turf

Turf can be laid during winter but avoid doing this in periods of extreme cold and frost as it may become impossible to prepare the underlying soil properly.

Picking up leaves

In mild conditions any remaining fallen leaves should be removed as they block out the light, killing the lawn. Leaves can be sucked up with a mower or raked up and added to the compost heap.

Once you have raked up fallen leaves, shred them using a rotary mower and add them to the compost.

During mild spells in winter, dig over areas that are going to become lawn, in preparation for laying the turf in spring.

Watering, feeding, and top-dressing

To keep a lawn looking healthy and green all year round it will need regular care and attention. Watering, feeding, and top-dressing are the three essential tasks required to create a lawn that will be the envy of your neighbours.

Drought During periods of drought grass stops growing, the blades turn yellow and then brown, before dying back exposing patches of soil. However, due to environmental concerns, lawns really only need watering in extremely dry conditions. Lawns can recover quickly after drought and often make a full and rapid recovery when rain appears. If lawns must be watered, do so in the morning or evening to reduce evaporation loss.

Watering tips If you want a very lush green lawn, your soil type will determine how often to water. Water once a week for clay and loamy soils and twice a week for sandy soils; water needs to penetrate down to the root systems – about 10cm (4in) down. A small inspection hole can be dug to check the moistness of the soil. Avoid spraying paths, patios, and hard surfaces to avoid water wastage.

Watering methods

Sprinklers In order to save time, large lawns are best irrigated with sprinklers, which can be timer-controlled to prevent water waste. There are various types available including oscillating sprinklers (*see above*), which spray from side to side, and rotary arm sprinklers that spray the full 360 degrees. If you have a small lawn, you may want to use a hand-held hosepipe with a spray attachment.

Watering can If you only have a small area of lawn, you may wish to water your grass using a watering can. Although filling and lifting a watering can requires greater effort than using a hose, you are likely to waste less water by doing this. If you have recently sown grass seed, use a rose on the end of the watering can's spout to make sure that seed is not washed away.

Feeding methods

Fertilizer There are three essential ingredients to look for when selecting a mineral fertilizer for your lawn: nitrogen (N), phosphorus (P), and potassium (K), which are usually expressed as a ratio of N:P:K. Nitrogen promotes rapid green growth and so is often found in high quantities in spring feeds. Phosphorus is used to promote root growth and so is often present in high amounts in autumn feeds and pre-seeder fertilizer. Potassium toughens up the grass making it resistant to disease, drought, and low temperatures and so is often high in autumn feeds. One other key ingredient to look out for is iron (Fe) which keeps the grass looking green without promoting excess growth. Blends of fertilizers and weedkillers can also be used, such as lawn sand (containing sulphate of ammonia, iron sulphate, and fine sand), which kills moss and weeds while at the same time acting as a feed for the grass.

Fertilizers can be spread by hand (wearing gloves) or using a drop spreader or cyclone spreader for larger areas.

Natural and liquid feeds As well as man-made fertilizers there are natural, organic materials that can be used to feed your lawn. A mulch mower chops up grass clippings and distributes them back onto the lawn thereby returning nitrogen to the soil. Bonemeal makes a useful phosphorus feed and liquid seaweed is high in iron. Liquid feeds enter the plant through the leaves giving quicker results than dry fertilizers, which dissolve in the soil and are then absorbed by the roots.

Top-dressing Applying top-dressing to your lawn improves the quality of the soil, levels out surface bumps and hollows, and fills the holes created by aeration. Ready-made mixes are available but you can make your own using sand, loam, and organic matter at a ratio of 3:3:1. Top-dressing should be spread evenly across the lawn and then brushed into aeration holes using a besom or broom. Ideally you should top-dress your lawn annually in autumn.

Feed young plants using a can with a fine rose.

Spread top-dressing evenly.

Brush into the lawn surface.

Lawn tools

Good quality tools are essential for ensuring a healthy lawn and using the right tool for the right job will make creation and maintenance simple. As well as common garden tools there are many specialist lawn tools that are designed to make lawn care easy.

Lawnmower This is the essential tool for any lawn. Different types are available, with rotary or cylinder blades (*see p.97*), and some collect grass clippings as they go. Mowers can be petrol driven; more environmentally friendly types run on batteries or are push-propelled.

Strimmer Essential for cutting grass that the mower can't reach, strimmers are excellent for use around walls, fences, and patios. They are also useful for banks, tight corners, and very long grass. They cut the blades of grass with nylon string that rotates at high speed (*see p.97*).

Edging shears A neatly edged lawn makes an attractive feature in the garden and edging shears make trimming easy. Push the soil away from the grass edge and then use the shears like scissors – only the cutting blade should move, while the other blade remains static.

Turfing iron This useful tool is used to remove turf from existing lawns. After the square of turf has been cut, the turfing iron is used to slice underneath it, severing the grass roots. It has a sharp point for cutting and an angled handle to produce level pieces of turf.

Half moon cutter Used for creating sharp, crisp edges or neat cuts, the half moon cutter is designed to slice efficiently through the turf with a flat blade that ensures a straight line. When cutting an edge, pull a line of string taut and follow it with the blade, chopping downwards.

Lawn tools *continued*

Broom (*right*) Good for a variety of uses, a broom is a common garden tool. Using a stiff broom is one of the most effective methods of brushing top-dressing into the holes created by aeration (although brooms with softer heads should be used on finer lawns). Brooms are also useful for sweeping hard surfaces such as paths and patios after lawn renovations, and for keeping the garden tidy.

Besom (*far right*) Often referred to as a witch's broom, this is a useful alternative to a stiff broom as the coarse brushwood is effective for sweeping leaves off the surface of the lawn in autumn, removing grass clippings after mowing, and sweeping top-dressing into the holes after aeration. Besoms are easy to make: tie brushwood (usually birch) to a stout wooden stick such as hazel using string.

Levelling rake (*far left*) Sometimes called landscape rakes, these large rakes can be bought with either wooden or stainless steel heads. When preparing the ground for laying turf or seed sowing they are used for the general levelling of the soil, usually after it has been dug over or rotavated. To get a smoother finish, the head of the rake can be turned over and run over the surface of the soil.

Spring-tined rake (*left*) These wire-tined rakes are used to remove the dead pieces of grass at the base of the plants, known as thatch. They should be used to vigorously scratch at the surface of the soil and should be used twice, in two different directions (the thatch can then be gathered up using a wide-headed plastic rake). Spring-tined rakes can also be used to remove leaves from the lawn.

Switch (*right*) A long, extended "whippy" rod, a switch is brushed over the grass in a circular sweeping motion to remove the dew each morning and to help dry out the lawn – running a bamboo cane horizontally over the surface of the lawn can have the same effect. This action is performed to deter fungus and diseases, which thrive in moist conditions, and it is also beneficial as having a dry lawn makes mowing easier. An alternative popular tool to reduce damp fungal problems is a dew brush, which is also used to sweep the morning moisture off the lawn. Drying the lawn is particularly important in shady areas where the sun won't dry the lawn naturally.

Aerating the lawn

Best performed lightly in spring or in autumn, lawn aeration is necessary to relieve soil compaction and to allow air to circulate around the grass roots and at the base of the leaf blades. There are various tools that can be used to achieve this from the simple garden fork to mechanical aerators that are ideal for use over large areas.

Fork Soil compaction can be relieved by pushing the solid tines of a fork into the lawn down to a depth of about 8cm (3in) and wiggling the fork slightly to widen the holes before continuing this process every 10cm (4in).

Hollow tiner This special tool is used in the same way as the fork (*left*) and using the same spacing, but it has hollow tines, meaning that cores of soil are removed, which should be filled in with good quality top-dressing.

Scarifier This tool removes leaves and any thatch at the base of the grass blades, allowing air to circulate and helping water and fertilizer to penetrate the root zone.

Spiked boots Combine a stroll in the garden with aerating the lawn: these strap-on soles have long spikes on the underneath that break up soil compaction as you walk.

Slitter A useful aeration alternative, the slitter is run over the grass and its sharp blades penetrate through the turf. It lightly trims the roots, allowing air to enter the root area.

Basic mowing techniques

Mowing is the most important maintenance job that your lawn requires. Regular mowing encourages healthy new growth and a strong root system to combat drought. It reduces a build-up of pests and diseases, and prevents weeds from seeding in the lawn and flowerbeds. Most importantly, a neatly mown lawn can lift the entire garden and make it look beautiful.

MOWING GUIDELINES		
SEASON	**UTILITY LAWN**	**HIGH QUALITY LAWN**
Spring and autumn	25mm (1in), once a week	8–10mm (3/8–1/2in), once or twice a week
Summer	15–20mm (1/2–1in), once a week	7–8mm (1/4–3/8in), up to three times a week
Winter	30mm (1 1/4in), as necessary	15mm (1/2in), as necessary

Mowing patterns

Mowing should be done regularly. It's best to remove small amounts of grass often rather than a lot in one cut. When mowing, start by cutting the outside edges first and then mow in straight lines up and down the centre. At the ends where the mower is turned it is worth leaving a double width strip. When the centre is finished, these ends should be re-mown to tidy up any missed patches – this is known as the "finishing strip". Alternate the direction in which you cut the lawn each time as otherwise ridges can form, particularly if you are using a mower with an attached roller. Consider mowing the lawn diagonally – this gives a neat finish and is an attractive alternative to going up and down its length.

Striped mowing patterns don't always have to be straight. Curved lines can create an interesting alternative and can be useful when mowing around curved flowerbeds, ponds, and circular patios.

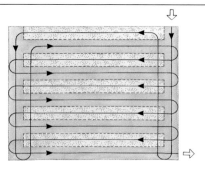

The path of a mower on a rectangular lawn.

Types of cut

There are essentially two types of lawn mower, giving two different types of cut: rotary and cylinder. With both kinds it is essential that the blades are kept sharp and are balanced properly, otherwise they will cut badly, leaving ragged tips on the blades of grass, making the lawn susceptible to disease. Mechanical mowers and strimmers should be serviced once a year if they are to give their best performance.

Rotary mowers The rotating blades slash through grass at high speed. Rotary mowers don't usually give as fine a finish as cylinder mowers but those with rollers attached to the back give a perfectly adequate cut and create attractive stripes. Mowing heights are usually easy to adjust.

Cylinder mowers With a cylinder structure that sits horizontal to the ground, this mower has a series of blades that spin, cutting against a static bottom blade. It gives a fine cut and is suitable for formal lawns or sports surfaces where a high quality finish is required.

Strimmers These are useful for cutting areas of long rough grass or for use on banks that are too steep to use a mower on. They operate by cutting with nylon strings, which spin at high speed. Strimmers often give a poor finish, leaving ragged tips that eventually go brown and die back.

What to do with clippings

Cutting a lawn regularly means there is no shortage of grass clippings to add to the compost heap each week. Small quantities should be added to the heap in alternate layers with other garden material as the clippings are very high in nitrogen and can turn slimy and smelly if left in bulk to rot down. Carbon-rich compost such as woody material, cardboard, or shredded newspaper should be added to the pile as well, as this will counterbalance the nitrogen from the clippings. The heap should be turned every few weeks to get air circulating inside the compost – this aids the breakdown of the material and will speed up the process. Bear in mind that clippings decompose better if they have been allowed to dry out first.

Maintaining a neat edge

Neat lawn edges give the garden structure and provide clear definition between the grass and any ornamental planting. Without these a design can be quickly lost to ragged edges, invasion of weeds, or a blurring of spaces.

Prune overhanging borders Ornamental border plants such as this geranium can rapidly spill onto the lawn if they are not kept in check. Plants like this need regular pruning as otherwise the grass underneath them will die, revealing bare earth in wintertime.

Use a half moon cutter Half moon cutters are used to create a distinctive edge between the lawn and flowerbeds. Pull a line of string taut from one end of the flowerbed to the other and then use the half moon cutter to slice down through the turf, following the line of the string. The half moon cutter has a flat blade surface that makes straight lines easy and a sharp edge, which allows the blade to cut cleanly through the turf; ensure that the blade is inserted straight or slightly angled outwards, otherwise the lawn edge may be prone to collapse. Avoid using a spade for cutting as the blade is slightly curved and will leave a scalloped finish. Add the turf cuttings to the compost.

Trim with edging shears Edging shears are used to cut the blades of grass that overhang the edges of the lawn. They have long handles and some of them are adjustable so you don't strain your back. Lawns should be edged immediately after mowing; if lawns are edged before mowing, the cutting can push blades of grass out to the side again. When cutting, only move the top blade as the lower blade should remain static – the action is like a pair of scissors. Move in the direction of the open end of the blades. Never leave the grass clippings in the gully between the border and the turf because they may seed or root into the soil. Instead use a rake to pick them up and add them to the compost heap.

Replace turf Often the edges of the lawn can crumble away, or die back, particularly if herbaceous plants have spread out over the lawn during the summer. The simplest solution is to cut out the affected area with a half moon cutter, slicing back to healthy turf. Remove the affected section and then rotate it 180 degrees, placing the healthy section of lawn on the edge. Then rake and re-seed the damaged area, which is now away from the lawn edge. Keep the replaced turf well watered during dry weather. Repeat this process wherever there are bare patches on the edge of the lawn.

Clearing and composting leaves

Leaves that fall onto the lawn in autumn must be collected up and removed to prevent the lawn from looking messy or worse, dying back from lack of light. However, the fallen leaves can easily be converted into rich, nutritious leafmould.

Removing leaves

The most effective method of removing leaves from the lawn is to use a rake to gather them up into small bundles and then add them to the general compost heap or put them aside to be used specifically for leafmould (*see facing page*). The best type of rake for doing this is a spring-tined rake (pictured) or a rake with a plastic head. The act of scraping up the leaves is in itself beneficial to the lawn, as it gives it a gentle scarification. There are various tools available to help make collecting up the leaves easier including large plastic "hands" or scoops with extended handles.

Clearing under trees

Leaves falling from deciduous trees onto the lawn can be problematic as this thick layer of mulch can kill the grass. To prevent this, create a circular bed around any trees, extending it to the edge of the leaf canopy. Fill it with shade-loving ground cover plants or spring-flowering bulbs that are capable of growing in shade and have adapted to growing under layers of leafmould. If you decide that you do want grass growing up to the trunk of the tree then remove the existing turf, prepare the ground well, removing any pernicious weeds, and re-sow the area with a shade-tolerant seed mix. Protect the grass seed with netting while it is germinating.

Making leafmould

1 Gather up any fallen deciduous leaves using a spring-tined rake. The leaves break down more quickly if shredded so run a rotary mower over them first if possible. Place them in dustbin liners or sturdy carrier bags.

2 Pour water over the leaves if they are dry as the moisture will speed up decomposition. Some leaves take longer to break down than others; leaves high in tannin such as oak and beech usually take the longest.

3 Puncture the bags with a fork or knife to allow air to circulate in the bag. The air assists in the breakdown of the leaves. Leave the bags out of sight, giving them an occasional shake and adding more water.

4 After one or two years the leafmould will be ready to use in the garden. It should make a lovely soil conditioner for borders, particularly around shade-loving plants, and is also a useful potting compost ingredient.

Levelling bumps and hollows

A lawn will need regular attention if it is to be an attractive feature in the garden. It may need repairing for a variety of reasons including wear and tear, drought, mole activities, or if frosts lift the turf. If bumps or hollows appear, follow these steps to keep your lawn level.

1 Regularly check over the lawn looking for any dips or hollows. Using a half moon cutter, slice a cross shape right through the centre of the hollow and beyond its edges, making the cut as even as possible.

2 With a turfing iron or a spade, cut under the turf using a slicing motion. The cut should be about 4–5cm (1½–2in) deep and the spade should be kept as flat as possible to keep the turf at an even thickness.

3 Peel back the four flaps of turf, being careful not to break them. If the soil is dry, lightly water the grass beforehand. If you are levelling a bump, dig out the soil until it is level with the surrounding area and proceed to step six.

Levelling bumps and hollows *continued*

4 If you are filling a hollow, fork over the soil to a depth of 5cm (2in) to break up any compaction or large clods. Remove any large stones. After digging, tread it down lightly, otherwise it will sink again after repairing.

5 Fill in the hollow using a good quality top-dressing until it is level with the surrounding soil. Rake it over to break the soil down to a fine tilth and then add more if necessary. Add a pre-seeder fertilizer to the soil.

6 Gently fold back the flaps of turf and firm them down by tamping them with the back of a rake. Start at the edges of the square and work your way into the centre. Do a final check to ensure that the ground is now level.

7 Finally, brush good quality top-dressing into the cracks to prevent the edges of the turf drying out. Lawn seed can be sprinkled into the gaps to fill them. The lawn should then be watered to help it establish.

Other lawn repairs

Replacing a square of turf When replacing a damaged patch of grass it is a good idea to try to identify the underlying cause so that you can try to prevent it from occurring again. For example, if the turf has become worn from being regularly walked on, it might be worth replacing it with a path or inserting stepping stones. The best time to repair damaged turf is autumn or spring. Cut out the slice of damaged turf using a half moon cutter, then use a turfing iron or spade to cut underneath, severing the roots, at a depth of about 4–5cm (1½–2in). Use a fork to dig over the bottom of the hole. Cut a new piece of turf from another area with similar grasses in it and tamp it down with the back of a rake. Water in well.

Re-seeding a patch of grass The best time to re-seed patches in the lawn is in spring or autumn. Fork over any bare areas of soil and then rake them level with the existing lawn. If the level is lower, build them up with top-dressing. Sprinkle grass seed at the supplier's recommended rate and then rake it in gently. Try to choose a seed mix that is suitable for your conditions. The grass might have suffered in the first place if the wrong mix was used; there are seed mixes for shady spots, high impact areas, and damp soils, so make sure you choose one that matches your conditions. Keep the areas well watered during germination and use netting to protect them from falling leaves and to deter birds.

Repairing patches Lawns can often start to look patchy and die back when they are growing in the shade. This frequently occurs under trees, near the edges of raised beds, or where edging material overshadows the turf. These areas will need regular repairs to keep them looking good. Remove the damaged sections of the lawn using a half moon cutter or spade and rake the area using top-dressing to adjust the level. Then sow a seed mix containing shade-tolerant species and water in well. Alternatively, repair the lawn using patches of turf from other areas of the lawn. Identify shady areas of the lawn that are already growing well, remove small sections of it, and use these to patch up the damaged area.

Cutting meadow grass

Meadows can provide a spectacular display of wildflowers and seedheads throughout the summer, but for this to continue year after year they will need an annual cut. Choose a dry day towards the end of summer.

Tip for success

Before cutting down a meadow, shake any ripe seedheads onto the ground. This should ensure that there are plenty of seeds in the ground for the following year.

1 Cut down the grasses and wildflowers using a scythe, being extremely careful to keep the blade well away from your body. Make sure that the blade is sharp, and cut the grass at a height of about 6cm (2½in).

2 Use a landscape rake to collect the cut grass into piles. It is worth leaving these clippings on the ground for a few days before you remove them, to allow any extra seed to drop and to allow any resident wildlife to escape.

Alternatives

3 Remove the cut grass after a few days as it can cause a thatch to form that may smother plants. Left clippings can also increase the soil fertility, which will encourage coarser grasses to compete with any wildflowers.

For smaller areas, it may be just as easy to use a pair of hand shears to cut back the meadow grass to the desired height. Alternatively for much larger areas of meadow, strimmers are very effective and will require less time and physical effort than a scythe.

Weeding

Although a few weeds can be tolerated in most lawns, and may be valuable for increasing the garden's biodiversity and for attracting beneficial insects such as bees and butterflies, many can look unsightly and may spread quickly if you do not deal with them promptly.

Why weed?

Some weeds will rapidly take over a lawn if they are not dealt with properly. Many of them are more vigorous than grasses and can quickly smother them. Also, weeds such as dandelions can rapidly colonize nearby flowerbeds if they are allowed to spread and annual weeds often fade away to leave bare patches of soil in the lawn. Finally, some weeds, such as thistles, are uncomfortable to sit or walk on. Knowing what type of weed you are dealing with will help you choose the best method of control.

Types of weed

Annuals Although weeds such as groundsel and chickweed germinate, flower, and die within one year, they can rapidly colonize a garden with their large numbers of seeds. It is best to hand-weed them as they have less extensive roots than perennial types.

Bulbil-producing Plants such as *Oxalis* (*shown above*) and buttercups build up a vigorous network of bulbils (small, bulb-like structures) in the soil, which can be difficult to remove. Chemical weedkillers are often the only effective method of control.

Perennials Common lawn weeds such as dandelions, daisies, and thistles (*shown above*) appear year after year. Most have extensive root systems making them hard to eradicate – remove the entire root as any pieces left in the ground will re-grow.

Controlling weeds

Weed-suppressing mulch Covering soil with weed-suppressing membrane is an effective method of preventing weeds from germinating. This is useful for bare soil but should not be used on lawns as it will kill the grass. It can also be used to warm the ground prior to sowing grass seed.

Preparatory spraying Drenching the soil with contact weedkiller prior to sowing prevents weed seeds from germinating. This should only be used on bare soil and not directly on lawns. Specific dilution and spraying rates should be strictly followed according to the label.

Fork Removing weeds with a fork is a useful method as it generally avoids chopping through perennial roots, which helps to propagate them. Hand forks can be used for clumps within the lawn whereas large forks should only be used for weeding large areas in preparation for grass seed or turf.

Daisy grubber This useful tool is pushed deep into the soil and then levered, prising out persistent perennial weeds such as daisies and dandelions with their tap roots intact. Due to its slender, compact shape the grubber causes minimal damage to the lawn when inserted.

Selective weedkiller Designed to be sprayed on lawns, these chemicals kill broadleaved weeds without harming the grass. Chemicals can either be bought ready to spray or they will need to be diluted beforehand. Always wear protective clothing.

Systemic weedkiller Brushing or wiping weedkiller onto individual weeds in the lawn can be a laborious process but is useful for spot-treating small areas. The chemicals are taken in through the leaf and down into the root system, killing the plant.

Common weeds

Yarrow
(*Achillea millefolium*)

This common weed bears clusters of creamy white flowers and has narrow, feather-like foliage which releases an aroma when crushed. It thrives in dry, arid, sandy conditions and often indicates a lack of nutrients in the soil. Pull out the rhizomes by hand.

H: 50cm (20in); **S**: 30cm (12in)

Daisy
(*Bellis perennis*)

The most common perennial weed in lawns, daisies have white petals and a yellow centre. They have green, spoon-shaped leaves that form clusters of rosettes in the grass. They are very resilient to close mowing, so use a daisy grubber to remove them.

H: 8cm (3in); **S**: 15cm (6in)

Creeping thistle
(*Cirsium arvense*)

This weed is often a problem in recently seeded lawns or in bare patches in existing swards. It has light purple flowerheads and spiky, wavy, thistle-like leaves, which are unpleasant to sit or walk on. Dig them out using a daisy grubber or fork.

H: 1.2m (4ft); **S**: 45cm (18in)

Ground ivy
(*Glechoma hederacea*)

This persistent, spreading perennial bears clusters of violet-blue flowers that are held high above the round, glossy, scalloped leaves. The aromatic foliage has pronounced veins and surrounds the stems. If necessary, apply an appropriate weedkiller.

H: 25cm (10in); **S**: 40cm (16in)

Greater plantain
(*Plantago major*)

This perennial has broad, oval-shaped foliage with pronounced rib markings; the leaves will rapidly smother the grass underneath them. The flowers are pale greenish-grey, borne on single stems. Dig it out, then mow regularly to prevent the seed spreading.

H: 15cm (6in); **S**: 20cm (8in)

Selfheal
(*Prunella vulgaris*)

A member of the mint family, this perennial can rapidly colonize a lawn using its spreading, underground runners. It has attractive, purplish-blue hooded flowers, and the leaves are borne in pairs along its squarish stems. Apply an appropriate weedkiller.

H: 20cm (8in); **S**: 30cm (12in)

Creeping buttercup
(*Ranunculus repens*)
Preferring damp soils, the buttercup is a good indicator that drainage may be required. It rapidly spreads using its creeping root system and has small, bright yellow flowers borne on erect stems, with three-lobed, toothed foliage. Dig out established plants.

H: 60cm (24in); **S**: 45cm (18in)

Sheep's sorrel
(*Rumex acetosella*)
A lover of dry, acidic soil conditions, this common perennial has unusual, arrow-shaped leaves and produces small, green flowers that turn to pinkish-red seedheads. Ensure that you dig out the entire tap root to prevent the plant regenerating.

H: 25cm (10in); **S**: 40cm (16in)

Common ragwort
(*Senecio jacobaea*)
This biennial weed bears bluish-green lobed leaves and bright yellow, star-shaped flowers. It seeds prolifically and so should be removed with a fork at an early stage of its growth. Because of the toxins it produces, wear gloves when weeding.

H: 80cm (32in); **S**: 25cm (10in)

Dandelion
(*Taraxacum officinale*)
Producing single, bright yellow flowerheads that turn into balls of white, fluffy seedheads, this perennial weed has shiny, elongated, toothed rosettes of foliage. Its deep, fleshy tap root needs to be removed completely otherwise it will rapidly regenerate.

H: 30cm (12in); **S**: 20cm (8in)

White clover
(*Trifolium repens*)
A common weed, often found on nutrient-rich soil, white clover has small, three-lobed leaves and white or sometimes pinkish flowers. It is a perennial weed and spreads by runners that can quickly smother the lawn; lift these with a rake, then mow.

H: 20cm (8in); **S**: 40cm (16in)

Slender speedwell
(*Veronica filiformis*)
This perennial has kidney-shaped leaves when young that develop into rounded, serrated foliage. Similar in appearance to ground ivy, it also bears blue-purplish flowers. It spreads by underground and overground runners; kill it using a hoe.

H: 10cm (4in); **S**: 50cm (20in)

Pests and diseases

Lawns can become vulnerable to pests and diseases for many reasons, including restricted air movement, poor drainage, a lack or excess of nutrients, and incorrect soil pH. There are also some grass species that are more susceptible, and some weather conditions that are simply more favourable for attack.

A healthy lawn Prevention is better than cure and with limited chemical treatments available to the amateur it is best to try to reduce the risk of pest and disease attacks wherever possible. Regular mowing keeps the grass healthy and strong, while removing the clippings helps to prevent a build-up of fungal spores. Avoid high nitrogen feeds during autumn as this encourages long, lush growth that is more susceptible to snow mould, rust, and other fungal diseases.

Disease prevention Most fungal diseases are caused by poor air circulation and damp conditions. The risk can be reduced by regularly scarifying the lawn to remove the thatch (dead grass), allowing air to circulate through the sward. Air circulation can also be improved by pruning overhanging trees and shrubs. Using a switch on the lawn will help remove excess dampness (*see p.94*), while aeration will reduce compaction and help air to reach the roots (*see p.95*).

Slime mould

Commonly found in late summer and autumn, slime moulds don't actually cause harm to the grass, although they are unsightly and unpleasant if sat on. There isn't a cure for the problem although regular aeration and scarifying reduce the risk of most fungi on the lawn. They can be removed immediately by spraying with a jet of water.

Red thread

Probably the most common lawn disease, red thread causes patches of red-tinged grass, which turn brown and die back. It is often associated with nitrogen deficiency so feed the lawn with ammonium sulphate as soon as symptoms are spotted; it is usually worst after wet summers and autumns. Regularly aerate and scarify to improve air circulation.

Rust

This disease can spread rapidly through a lawn creating yellow patches. Up close, rusty orange pustules can be seen on the grass blades. No chemical control is available, but regular mowing and the removal of clippings will prevent it spreading. Avoid using high nitrogen fertilizers in autumn as this can cause lank growth, which is more susceptible to disease.

Snow mould (Fusarium patch)

Most commonly seen in autumn or after snow, this fungal disease appears as yellow or brownish patches on the lawn, occasionally with a layer of white or sometimes pink mould that looks similar to cobwebs. Patches can spread rapidly and destroy a lawn. Scarification can help reduce the risk, as can avoiding high nitrogen feeds in autumn.

Ant nests

Ant hills look unsightly on a lawn and if they cannot be tolerated consider using the nematode *Steinernema feltiae* as a biological control, which is available from mail order companies. The proprietary ant powders and sprays available for controlling ants are usually for use in buildings and not effective outdoors where ant nests can be deep in the soil.

Chafer grubs

These unattractive grubs are the larvae of the chafer beetle and cause problems not only because they feed on grass roots but also because creatures such as badgers and birds often tear the lawn up in order to eat them. Biological control involves watering in nematodes, which are available by mail order, although chemical controls are also available.

Fairy rings

These often appear as irregular dead circles in the lawn or as a ring of toadstools. Effective chemical controls are only available to professionals, so the only possible solution, which is not always feasible, is to dig out the affected area to a depth of 30cm (12in) and replace it with healthy top soil before seeding or turfing the surface.

Leatherjackets

These are the larval stage of crane flies, or daddy-longlegs, and cause yellow or brown patches on the lawn surface as they eat through the roots below. To make it worse, birds may tear up the lawn as they attempt to dig down and feed on the larvae. To control, cover the lawn with plastic to draw the larvae to the surface and then allow the birds to feed on them.

Moles

The underground tunnelling of moles as they search for worms and grubs leads to the creation of mole hills as the soil is deposited on the surface of the lawn. This makes mowing difficult, creates bare soil for weeds to germinate in, and destabilizes the lawn. Placing mole traps in the tunnels is the only effective method of control.

Worm casts

The casts left by worms on the lawn surface are an unsightly mess. They should be brushed off when dry as otherwise they will be smeared during mowing and this kills the grass underneath them, leaving bare soil for weeds to germinate in. Don't overwater a lawn as worms love moist conditions. Use a switch regularly to remove excess moisture.

Plant guide

This comprehensive guide will provide you with information on key lawn and meadow grasses, wildflowers, bulbs, and ground cover to help you pick the most suitable plants for your site. The symbols below are used in this chapter to indicate the conditions that each plant requires.

Key to plant symbols

♀   Plants given the RHS Award of Garden Merit

Soil preference

◊   Well-drained soil

◐   Moist soil

◆   Wet soil

Preference for sun or shade

☼   Full sun

☀   Partial or dappled shade

☀   Full shade

Hardiness ratings

✲✲✲   Fully hardy plants

✲✲   Plants that survive outside in mild regions or sheltered sites

✲   Plants that need protection from fro over winter

Lawn grasses

Agrostis capillaris
Browntop bent is used in both fine lawns and wildflower meadows. It is highly regarded due to its fine leaves and attractive appearance. It is often combined with fescues when used in formal settings and it tolerates low mowing down to 3 or 4mm (⅛in).

H: 50cm (20in); **S**: 30cm (12in)
❀❀❀ ☼ ☀ ◌ ◑

Festuca ovina
Often found in the pasture fields of grazing sheep, the densely tufted sheep's fescue is also found in lawn mixes. It has good drought resistance and thrives in well-drained, slightly acidic soils with poor fertility. It has bristly, grey-green leaves.

H: 40cm (16in); **S**: 15cm (6in)
❀❀❀ ☼ ☀ ◌

Festuca rubra
Its slender, needle-like blades make slender creeping red fescue a desirable species for a formal lawn. As the name suggests, it has a creeping habit, creating dense coverage. Combine it with *Agrostis capillaris* for the ideal formal lawn.

H: 50cm (20in); **S**: 15cm (6in)
❀❀❀ ☼ ☀ ◌ ◑

Holcus lanatus
Yorkshire fog is a very vigorous, coarse grass and although common in many lawns, is not usually desirable due to its unattractive thick, coarse, hairy leaves. In meadows it tends to out-compete wildflowers, although it does bear attractive seedheads.

H: 80cm (32in); **S**: 25cm (10in)
❀❀❀ ☼ ☀ ◌ ◑

Lolium perenne

The tough, resilient, fast-growing rye grass is commonly used for sports pitches and family lawns. Traditionally it is cut no lower than 30mm (1¼in), but new fine-leaved, dwarf varieties can be cut to 5mm (¼in), giving the appearance of a fine lawn species.

H: 80cm (32in); **S**: 25cm (10in)
❀❀❀ ☼ ☀ ◊

Phleum pratense

Timothy grass bears coarse, tufted, broad leaves and attractive, densely packed flowerheads, up to 15cm (6in) long. It is hard-wearing, so is suitable for areas that receive a lot of wear and tear but it won't tolerate low mowing, so is unsuitable for formal situations.

H: 1m (3ft); **S**: 25cm (10in)
❀❀❀ ☼ ☀ ◊ ◖

Agrostis stolonifera

Creeping bent is a popular perennial grass and commonly found in lawn mixes. It grows in a wide range of locations including grassland, chalk downlands, and open woodland. It has a creeping habit, creating a tightly knitted lawn structure.

H: 30cm (12in); **S**: 15cm (6in)
❀❀❀ ☼ ☀ ◊ ◖

Festuca arundinacea

Often known as rhizomatous tall fescue, or RTF, this lawn grass is becoming increasingly popular in public gardens and sports stadiums; its deep-rooting rhizomes make it tolerant of compaction, drought, and waterlogging. Mow to 20mm (¾in).

H: 60cm (24in); **S**: 20cm (8in)
❀❀❀ ☼ ☀ ◊ ◖

Festuca rubra subsp. commutata

Clump-forming chewing's fescue has a fine, needle-like structure with high shoot density. Easy to establish, it can be closely mown, and maintains good year-round colour. It has some shade tolerance and disease resistance.

H: 40cm (16in); **S**: 15cm (6in)
❀❀❀ ☼ ☀ ◊ ◖

Poa annua

Annual meadow grass is common in lawns but is often considered to be a weed. The grass is attractive when in full leaf, but can produce a lot of seedheads at a very low height, fade quickly to yellow, and then die, leaving bare soil in its place.

H: 25cm (10in); **S**: 10cm (4in)
❀❀❀ ☼ ☀ ◊ ◖

Poa pratensis

Known as smooth-stalked meadow grass or Kentucky blue grass, this is often combined with rye grass in family lawn mixes, amenity lawns, and sports fields due to its resistance to wear and tear. It is a good choice for play areas, banks, and slopes.

H: 65cm (26in); **S**: 20cm (8in)
❀❀❀ ☼ ☀ ◊ ◖

Poa trivialis

As its name suggests, rough-stalked meadow grass is a coarse variety and can often be found in sports field and family lawn mixtures as it is hard-wearing and durable. It is also commonly found in meadows and pasture land with rich soil.

H: 50cm (20in); **S**: 15cm (6in)
❀❀❀ ☼ ☀ ◊ ◖

Meadow grasses

Anthoxanthum odoratum
This short-growing meadow grass is one of the first to flower, producing an attractive brownish-yellow flower spike in mid-spring. Its common name – sweet vernal grass – refers to the vanilla scent released when it is cut for hay.

H: 30cm (12in); **S**: 30cm (12in)
✿✿✿ ◊ ◖ ☼ ☀

Briza media
One of the most attractive meadow grasses, quaking grass produces delicate, pendent, purplish-green flower spikes that appear to tremble in the wind. The green seedheads slowly turn yellow over the summer months. It prefers alkaline soils.

H: 40cm (16in); **S**: 50cm (20in)
✿✿✿ ◊ ◖ ☼ ☀

Cynosurus cristatus
A common grassland species, crested dog's tail has a slightly tufted habit and is tolerant of poor, infertile soils. It has attractive, light green foliage with elegant flower spikes. The seedheads are flat on one side, giving the grass a crested appearance.

H: 50cm (20in); **S**: 50cm (20in)
✿✿✿ ◊ ☼ ☀ ♉

Koeleria macrantha
Crested hair grass is commonly found in grassland habitats. It is a tufted perennial with long leaf blades; like *Cynosurus cristatus*, the seedhead is flat on one side, making it look as if it has a crest running up it. Its height can vary depending on its conditions.

H: 40cm (16in); **S**: 30cm (12in)
✿✿✿ ◊ ☼ ☀

Phleum bertolonii
The perennial smaller cat's tail tolerates a wide range of soil types from sand to clay, but particularly thrives in cool, moist conditions. It bears attractive cylindrical flowerheads and is very similar to *Phleum pratense*, only slightly smaller.

H: 30cm (12in); **S**: 30cm (12in)
✿✿✿ ◊ ◖ ☼ ☀

Trisetum flavescens
A medium-sized perennial, yellow oat grass prefers chalky soil and thrives in poor, infertile conditions. It has flat leaves and attractive delicate, yellow, oat-like flowerheads. It is more drought-tolerant than many other grasses.

H: 50cm (20in); **S**: 50cm (20in)
✿✿✿ ◊ ☼ ☀ ♉

Flowers for beneficial insects

Echium vulgare 'Blue Bedder'
Biennial viper's bugloss bears attractive pink buds that open to reveal blue flowers. It is one of the most popular plants for butterflies, bees, and other insects. It prefers chalky, light soils and is often found in undisturbed soil or coastal areas.

H: 50cm (20in); **S**: 40cm (16in)
❋❋❋ ◊ ☼ ☀

Leontodon hispidus
Commonly found on well-drained, chalky grassland, rough hawkbit bears a bright yellow flower that closely resembles that of a dandelion. The flower is held high on a single hairy stem with a cluster of hairy leaves at its base.

H: 35cm (14in); **S**: 20cm (8in)
❋❋❋ ◊ ◊ ☼ ☀

Lotus corniculatus
Bird's foot trefoil is a tough plant from the pea family that bears attractive double yellow flowers in spring and summer, which develop into small black pea pods. It tolerates a wide range of soil conditions and its height can vary depending on these.

H: 50cm (20in); **S**: 40cm (16in)
❋❋❋ ◊ ◊ ☼ ☀

Malva moschata
Producing a pale pink or white flower and feathery, dissected, kidney-shaped leaves, musk mallow is often found on waste ground, the edges of woodland, in grasslands, and in hedges. The foliage has a slightly musky scent and is used in traditional medicine.

H: 75cm (30in); **S**: 60cm (24in)
❋❋❋ ◊ ☼ ☀

Origanum vulgare
This is the wild form of marjoram, the popular kitchen herb, and is commonly found in grassland habitats in full sun. Belonging to the mint family, the foliage is highly aromatic and the purple buds develop into delicate bunches of pink or white flowers.

H: 50cm (20in); **S**: 50cm (20in)
❋❋❋ ◊ ☼ ☀

Trifolium pratense
A favourite with many species of bumblebee, wild red clover prefers grasslands and natural hay meadows. It can be problematic when grown among wildflowers as its roots fix nitrogen, increasing soil fertility and therefore swamping delicate flowers.

H: 40cm (16in); **S**: 30cm (12in)
❋❋❋ ◊ ◊ ☼ ☀

Perennials for wildflower meadows

Campanula latifolia
Also popular as a border plant, milky bellflower has an upright habit and bears purple-mauve, bell-shaped flowers. The serrated foliage is similar to an elongated nettle leaf, although it doesn't sting. It prefers hedgerows and dappled woodland habitat.

H: 1m (3ft); **S**: 60cm (24in)
❋❋❋ ○ ◐ ☼ ☀

Centaurea nigra
Common knapweed produces attractive pinkish-purple, thistle-like flowers and long, dissected leaves. Ideal for a wildlife garden, it is a useful source of nectar for insects, while its seedheads provide food for birds during winter.

H: 80cm (32in); **S**: 40cm (16in)
❋❋❋ ○ ◐ ☼ ☀

Centaurea scabiosa
A popular nectar source for bees and butterflies, greater knapweed bears pinkish-purple, thistle-like flowerheads held high over its long and often deeply divided foliage. It is very similar to common knapweed, but larger and with a more untidy habit.

H: 1m (3ft); **S**: 60cm (24in)
❋❋❋ ○ ◐ ☼ ☀

Daucus carota
Similar in appearance to cow parsley, wild carrot is commonly grown as a biennial. It bears lacy, umbelliferous flowers that are usually white but occasionally have a pinkish tinge. It prefers poor, free-draining soil; its tap root makes it drought-tolerant.

H: 75cm (30in); **S**: 70cm (28in)
❋❋❋ ○ ◐ ☼ ☀

Galium verum
Lady's bedstraw is an attractive plant, producing dense clusters of golden flowers held high on its unusual square stems. It is a low, scrambling plant that sends down roots wherever it comes into contact with the ground. The whole plant smells of hay.

H: 35cm (14in); **S**: 20cm (8in)
❋❋❋ ○ ◐ ☼ ☀

Geranium pratense

Meadow cranesbill, a wild form of geranium, bears attractive, veined, violet blue or white flowers and deeply divided, five- to seven-lobed leaves. It is frequently found in rough grassland, damp hay meadows, and lightly grazed pastures.

H: 75cm (30in); **S**: 50cm (20in)
❄❄❄ ◊ ◊ ☀ ☀

Knautia arvensis

Field scabious is a hairy biennial or perennial, bearing flowers in a range of colours from violet blue to pale lavender. The pin-cushion-shaped blooms are held high on a mass of branched stems. It is a popular source of nectar for butterflies and bees.

H: 60cm (24in); **S**: 50cm (20in)
❄❄❄ ◊ ◊ ☀ ☀

Lathyrus pratensis

Part of the pea family, scrambling meadow vetchling bears attractive yellow flowers throughout the summer that develop into black pea pods. The stems carry pairs of leaves and tendrils. It is commonly found in hedgerows and rough grassland.

H: 50cm (20in); **S**: 40cm (16in)
❄❄❄ ◊ ◊ ☀ ☀

Leucanthemum vulgare

A common site on banks, verges, and disturbed ground, the ox-eye daisy bears white flowers with deep yellow disc florets in the centres, on single stems. The foliage is dark green, spoon-shaped, toothed, and forms a rosette at the base of the plant.

H: 75cm (30in); **S**: 40cm (16in)
❄❄❄ ◊ ◊ ☀ ☀

Linaria vulgaris

Distinctive and attractive, toadflax bears tall, cylindrical spikes of pale yellow flowers with deep egg yolk-coloured centres – it is also commonly known as butter and eggs due to these contrasting colours. The foliage is narrow and greyish-green.

H: 40cm (16in); **S**: 30cm (12in)
❄❄❄ ◊ ◊ ☀ ☀

Annuals for wildflower meadows

Agrostemma githago
A beautiful summer-flowering annual, corn cockle bears large, five-petalled, magenta-coloured flowers and is often associated with arable fields. Once a common wildflower, it is scarcer now due to the practices of intensive agriculture.

H: 70cm (28in); **S**: 40cm (16in)
❄❄❄ ◊ ◐ ☼ ☀

Anthemis arvensis
Corn chamomile is a classic meadow plant bearing large, white, daisy-like flowerheads with yellow disc florets in the centre. It is ideal for naturalizing in wildflower meadows or as part of a corn mix with corn cockle, cornflowers, and corn marigolds.

H: 50cm (20in); **S**: 40cm (16in)
❄❄❄ ◊ ◐ ☼ ☀

Atriplex hortensis
An annual, edible crop, purple orache makes an interesting addition to any wildflower mix. It is a tall, erect plant, and its deep purple or reddish foliage and purple flower spikes create a striking contrast with neighbouring flowers.

H: 2m (6ft); **S**: 1m (3ft)
❄❄❄ ◊ ◐ ☼ ☀ ♀

Centaurea cyanus
Often found growing around the edges of arable fields, the beautiful annual cornflower has pastel blue outer petals with reddish purple inner florets. It used to be a common wildflower on farmland but its numbers are now in decline.

H: 60cm (24in); **S**: 40cm (16in)
❄❄❄ ◊ ◐ ☼ ☀

Coreopsis tinctoria
This stunning annual flower creates a bright, spectacular splash of colour in any annual wildflower meadow mix. It bears intense yellow, daisy-shaped flowers with bronze or mahogany-red centres, which bloom from mid- to late summer.

H: 60cm (24in); **S**: 40cm (16in)
❄❄❄ ◊ ◐ ☼

Eschscholzia californica
The fast-growing Californian poppy bears single flowerheads in a range of colours including orange, yellow, and red, followed by attractive curved seed pods. The poppies have feathery leaves and will self-seed year after year in annual flower mixes.

H: 40cm (16in); **S**: 20cm (8in)
❄❄❄ ◊ ◐ ☼ ♀

Glebionis segetum

Producing bright golden-yellow daisy-shaped flowers, the corn marigold is a popular choice. It is a useful plant due to its ferny, grey-green foliage and the instant impact given by its brightly coloured flowers, which have a long flowering period.

H: 70cm (28in); **S**: 45cm (18in)
❀❀❀ ◊ ◑ ☼

Helianthus annuus

The sunflower is a striking annual bearing large bright yellow flowers. There are many varieties to choose from, some growing over 2m (6ft) tall, but the smaller types are better suited to meadows. It is an "instant impact" plant that is easy to germinate.

H: 2m (6ft); **S**: 50cm (20in)
❀❀❀ ◊ ◑ ☼

Papaver rhoeas

A field full of bright scarlet red poppies with jet black centres held high on slender stems is a magnificent sight. The leaves are jagged and lobed and the seeds are often used in baking. Preferring disturbed ground, seeds can lie dormant for years.

H: 1m (3ft); **S**: 30cm (12in)
❀❀❀ ◊ ◑ ☼

Papaver somniferum

The large, blowsy flowerheads of the opium poppy make it a common choice in annual flower mixes. It has attractive blue-green leaves and the single or double flowers are borne in a range of colours including purple, red, and white.

H: 1.2m (4ft); **S**: 40cm (16in)
❀❀❀ ◊ ◑ ☼

Rhinanthus minor

Semi-parasitic yellow rattle is commonly used to reduce the vigour of competing coarse grasses in meadows, allowing other plants to grow. Yellow hooded flowers are followed by papery seedheads that rattle in the wind.

H: 30cm (12in); **S**: 15cm (6in)
❀❀❀ ◊ ☼

Verbena bonariensis

Verbena is actually a short-lived perennial, but in places with cold winters is treated as an annual. It is a tall, slender plant producing attractive flat-headed, lavender-purple flowers held high on multiple square stems. It is attractive to bees and butterflies.

H: 1.3m (4½ft); **S**: 40cm (16in)
❀❀❀ ◊ ☼ ♀

Woodland wildflowers

Agrimonia eupatoria
An upright perennial, agrimony produces long, yellow flower spikes. It frequently grows in hedgerows, grasslands, and roadside verges, and copes with dappled shade. It has a long history of use as a medicinal plant, particularly for healing wounds.

H: 50cm (20in); **S**: 30cm (12in)
✳✳✳ ◊ ☀

Alliaria petiolata
Also known as Jack-by-the-hedge, garlic mustard is commonly found in hedgerows and woodland edges. Its kidney-shaped, serrated, alternately spaced leaves smell mildly of garlic. It bears small, white clusters of flowers followed by long, ribbed seed pods.

H: 60cm (24in); **S**: 30cm (12in)
✳✳✳ ◊ ☀

Betonica officinalis
Preferring slightly acidic and damp soils, betony is a perennial that belongs to the dead-nettle family. Its serrated, oblong leaves grow in pairs along its square stem. It produces purple or occasionally white flower spikes.

H: 30cm (12in); **S**: 20cm (8in)
✳✳✳ ◊ ☀

Digitalis purpurea
A commonly seen woodland wildflower, the foxglove is a tall, slender biennial or short-lived perennial. It produces purplish-pink, tubular flowers with spots on the inside. The leaves, seeds, and flowers are poisonous to humans.

H: 1.2m (4ft); **S**: 40cm (16in)
✳✳✳ ◊ ☀

Filipendula ulmaria
Preferring damp, wet conditions, meadowsweet is a tall perennial that produces a mass of frothy-looking creamy flowers. It has a sweet scent and is commonly found in meadows but is equally tolerant of shady hedgerows and dappled shade.

H: 90cm (36in); **S**: 60cm (24in)
✳✳✳ ◊ ◊ ◆ ☼ ☀

Geum urbanum
Wood avens is a common woodland perennial, with small, yellow, five-petalled flowers and short, dark green leaves. Its roots are distinctively clove-scented. Seeds are spread by animals; the spiked crimson seeds hook onto them as they pass.

H: 40cm (16in); **S**: 30cm (12in)
✳✳✳ ◊ ☼ ☀

Lychnis flos-cuculi

A damp-loving plant, ragged robin is commonly found in wetlands, on pond margins, and in shady, open, wet woodland. It is an upright perennial, bearing loose clusters of pink flowers. The leaves are pale green and borne in pairs along its light red stems.

H: 1m (3ft); **S**: 60cm (24in)
❄❄❄ ◊ ● ☼ ☀

Primula veris

The cowslip is an attractive perennial wildflower that looks particularly striking when naturalized in grassland. Clusters of small, deep yellow, tubular flowers are held on long, thin, leafless stems. The dark green foliage grows in a rosette.

H: 30cm (12in); **S**: 20cm (8in)
❄❄❄ ◊ ● ☼ ☀ ♈

Primula vulgaris

The primrose is a compact, early-flowering perennial, bearing fragrant, pale yellow blooms with dark yellow centres, carried on delicate, pinkish stems. The plants are commonly found in deciduous woodlands, damp grassland, and scrub areas.

H: 20cm (8in); **S**: 30cm (12in)
❄❄❄ ◊ ☼ ☀ ♈

Silene dioica

Summer-flowering red campion thrives on woodland edges, shady banks, rich meadows, and hedgerows. It produces attractive deep pink flowers that are borne on long, branching stems. The matt green leaves are hairy and slightly oval.

H: 90cm (3ft); **S**: 30cm (12in)
❄❄❄ ◊ ● ☼ ☀

Stachys sylvatica

This medium-sized perennial is often found in deciduous woodland and alongside hedgerows in moist, fertile soil. Hedge woundwort produces distinctive whorls of purplish-pink flowers with white speckles. The foliage is aromatic and dark green.

H: 80cm (32in); **S**: 60cm (24in)
❄❄❄ ◊ ● ☀

Teucrium scorodonia

A member of the mint family, wood sage looks similar to common sage but is hairier and its leaves are more wrinkly. The pungent leaves are more reminiscent of hops than sage, and in the past were used to flavour beer. Its flowers are greenish yellow in colour.

H: 60cm (24in); **S**: 60cm (24in)
❄❄❄ ◊ ● ☀

Prairie meadow plants

Asclepias tuberosa
Native to the dry grasslands of North America, this upright, bulbous rooted perennial bears flat-topped clusters of bright orange flowers over a long period during summer. It has slightly fleshy, lance-shaped, light green leaves.

H: 75cm (30in); **S**: 50cm (20in)
❀❀❀ ◊ ☼

Echinacea purpurea
An upright, vigorous, easy-to-grow plant, the cone flower bears large, solitary, daisy-like flowers on thick, hairy stems during summer. The ray florets are light purple and slightly reflexed back, revealing the central orange-brown cone-shaped centre.

H: 1m (3ft); **S**: 1m (3ft)
❀❀❀ ◊ ☼

Eryngium yuccifolium
The sea holly has long, lance-shaped, spiny, glossy foliage and bears masses of tiny silvery white globes of flowers from midsummer to early autumn. Bees and butterflies love the plant and the striking flowers are ideal for flower arranging.

H: 1m (3ft); **S**: 1m (3ft)
❀❀❀ ◊ ☼

Eupatorium purpureum
An invaluable plant for impact in the late-summer border, this large herbaceous perennial grows up to 2m (6ft) high in fertile soil. The domed, pinkish-purple flowerheads are rich in nectar, making this plant attractive to butterflies and bees.

H: 2m (6ft); **S**: 1.5m (5ft)
❀❀❀ ◊ ☼

Helenium autumnale
An attractive late summer and autumn herbaceous perennial, sneezewort produces a fiery display of yellow and red-hued daisy-like flowers with prominent central discs. Cultivars provide mixes of colours such as orange, bronze, and brown.

H: 1.5m (5ft); **S**: 1.2m (4ft)
❀❀❀ ◊ ◐ ☼

Miscanthus sinensis 'Zebrinus'
This large ornamental grass forms clumps of long, graceful, arching leaves with bands of pale yellow stripes across them; it is ideal for the back of a prairie-style border. In favourable conditions it bears silvery-pink flowery plumes in late summer.

H: 2m (6ft); **S**: 1.2m (4ft)
❀❀❀ ◊ ◐ ☼ ◑ ♈

Molinia caerulea 'Karl Foerster'

This attractive form of purple moor grass is a clump-forming ornamental perennial with green foliage that turns golden yellow in autumn. A mass of purple flower spikes appear in late spring to summer. It is a good architectural and structural plant.

H: 80cm (32in); **S**: 60cm (24in)
❄❄❄ ◊ ◑ ☼ ☼

Monarda fistulosa

From mid- to late summer this perennial bears whorls of lilac flowers which are very attractive to bees. It has upright stems and green, aromatic, lance-shaped foliage. It does best in slightly moist soil in summer although it is intolerant of damp winters.

H: 1.2m (4ft); **S**: 45cm (18in)
❄❄❄ ◊ ◑ ☼

Rudbeckia subtomentosa

This herbaceous perennial is essential for prairie-style borders. Its flowers have bright yellow, daisy-like petals surrounding a darkly coloured central cone. It produces an abundance of blooms on masses of tall, upright stems in late summer.

H: 1m (3ft); **S**: 50cm (20in)
❄❄❄ ◊ ◑ ☼

Stipa tenuissima

A deciduous perennial, this compact and popular species of grass has fine, arching, green foliage. It produces masses of pale, feathery flowers that almost obscure the leaves, followed by seedheads in summer. The foliage should be cut back in autumn.

H: 80cm (32in); **S**: 60cm (24in)
❄❄❄ ◊ ◑ ☼ ☼

Verbena hastata

Blue vervain prefers a more moist soil than many traditional prairie-style schemes. It can become quite large in wet areas, growing up to 1.8m (6ft) tall. It produces mauve flower spikes and the foliage is green and serrated, borne on greenish-red stems.

H: 1m (3ft); **S**: 70cm (28in)
❄❄❄ ◑ ☼ ☼

Veronicastrum virginicum

A useful architectural and structural herbaceous perennial combining beautifully with ornamental grasses for loose ephemeral planting in the prairie border. This plant bears lots of pink, small, tubular flowers carried on long flower spires.

H: 1.3m (4½ft); **S**: 80cm (32in)
❄❄❄ ◊ ◑ ☼ ☼

Bulbs and corms for lawn areas

Allium moly
This easy-to-grow ornamental onion looks beautiful naturalized in a lawn. It is low growing and produces masses of bright yellow, star-shaped flowers during summer. The greyish-green, strap-shaped leaves release a subtle onion aroma when crushed.

H: 25cm (10in); **S**: 30cm (12in)
✻✻✻ ◊ ☼

Anemone blanda 'White Splendour'
Producing an abundance of flattish, white flowers with yellow centres, this spring-flowering perennial is easy to grow and can be planted under trees in lawns. The foliage is dark green and delicately lobed. It requires fertile soil.

H: 15cm (6in); **S**: 15cm (6in)
✻✻✻ ◊ ☼ ☼ ♀

Camassia quamash
A good choice for damp and wet grasslands, this bulbous, clump-forming perennial bears masses of purplish-blue or white, star-shaped flowers on upright stems. It makes a stunning display when planted *en masse* in wet meadows or lawns.

H: 50cm (20in); **S**: 20cm (8in)
✻✻✻ ◊ ◖ ☼ ☼

Chionodoxa 'Pink Giant'
Glory of the snow originates from Turkey. Its low-growing mass of large pink flowers with yellowish-white centres creates a spectacular carpet of colour in early spring. It is a good choice for naturalizing in lawns, rock gardens, and the edges of woodland.

H: 15cm (6in); **S**: 20cm (8in)
✻✻✻ ◊ ☼ ☼

Crocus 'Ruby Giant'
This early springtime flowering crocus can be planted in lawns and under trees. Despite its name, 'Ruby Giant' produces deep purple flowers with yellow centres, and long, mid-green leaves. Plant with autumn crocuses for a second display of colour.

H: 8cm (3in); **S**: 8cm (3in)
✻✻✻ ◊ ☼ ☼

Eranthis hyemalis
Ideal for naturalizing under trees, around shrub borders, and along the edges of hedgerows, this plant will bring a splash of colour to the winter garden. It has bright yellow, buttercup-shaped flowers and light green, strap-shaped leaves.

H: 8cm (3in); **S**: 8cm (3in)
✻✻✻ ◊ ◖ ☼ ♀

Fritillaria meleagris

Snake's head fritillary is particularly striking when seen *en masse* in damp meadowland. The bell-shaped flowerheads are pinkish-purple with a white chequered pattern. They hang on single stems with narrow, grey-green leaves at their base.

H: 30cm (12in); **S**: 8cm (3in)
❄❄❄ ◐ ☀

Galanthus nivalis

Heralding the beginning of spring, snowdrops are vigorous, bulbous perennials with drooping, pear-shaped, white flowerheads. They have narrow, grey-green leaves and are ideal for naturalizing in lawns under deciduous trees, shrubs, and hedges.

H: 10cm (4in); **S**: 10cm (4in)
❄❄❄ ◌ ◐ ☀ ☼ ♈

Leucojum aestivum

Often confused with snowdrops, the snowflake is a larger, taller plant that bears a green or yellow spot at the tip of each petal. The flowers are white, pear-shaped, and drooping, and are a good choice for rockeries and flower borders.

H: 50cm (20in); **S**: 20cm (8in)
❄❄❄ ◌ ◐ ☀ ☼

Narcissus bulbocodium

The bright yellow, trumpet-shaped, wide open flowers earn this plant the name "hoop petticoat daffodil". Like most daffodils it requires moist but well-drained soil. Daffodils are one of the most popular spring flowers for naturalizing in lawns and meadows.

H: 20cm (8in); **S**: 10cm (4in)
❄❄❄ ◌ ◐ ☀ ☼ ♈

Narcissus cyclamineus

Thriving in damp meadows, this cyclamen-flowered daffodil has a distinctive bright yellow pendent flowerhead surrounded by pale yellow petals. It is a vigorous, dwarf perennial and does best in moist but well-drained lawns.

H: 20cm (8in); **S**: 10cm (4in)
❄❄❄ ◌ ◐ ☀ ☼ ♈

Tulipa sprengeri

Originating from Turkey, this species tulip produces delicate, bright scarlet flowers with yellow centres, held high above its light green, strap-shaped leaves. It is the last tulip to flower in springtime so plant it with other bulbs for a long season of colour.

H: 50cm (20in); **S**: 30cm (12in)
❄❄❄ ◌ ☀ ☼ ♈

Ground cover for sun

Achillea filipendulina 'Gold Plate'

This traditional border plant is useful for covering expanses of the garden due to its large feathery foliage and wide, flat flowerheads. It produces bright golden flowerheads over 15cm (6in) across and combines well in meadow or prairie planting.

H: 1.2m (4ft); **S**: 45cm (18in)
❄❄❄ ◌ ◗ ☼ ☀ ♀

Alchemilla mollis

Coping with both dappled shade and full sun, lady's mantle has light green, ruffled, fan-shaped leaves and small, lime-green flowerheads. This attractive herbaceous perennial looks especially effective when used to underplant taller shrubs.

H: 60cm (24in); **S**: 45cm (18in)
❄❄❄ ◌ ◗ ☼ ☀ ♀

Anaphalis triplinervis

An herbaceous perennial with tiny white sprays of flowers, pearl everlasting has a neat, clump-forming, and spreading habit. It has attractive grey-green, thin, elliptical foliage and white hairy stems. It is ideal for the front of a sunny border.

H: 50cm (20in); **S**: 1m (3ft)
❄❄❄ ◌ ☼ ☀ ♀

Artemisia ludoviciana 'Silver Queen'

Commonly grown for its attractive, silvery white leaves rather than its insignificant late-summer, brown-yellow flowers, this semi-evergreen is a good foliage plant for gravel gardens or in Mediterranean borders.

H: 75cm (30in); **S**: 75cm (30in)
❄❄❄ ◌ ☼ ☀ ♀

Calluna vulgaris 'Peter Sparkes'

This heather produces dense clusters of bell-shaped, bright lilac flowers and grey-green foliage. It requires an acidic soil for successful growth. Heathers are popular with beekeepers as they have a reputation for providing the tastiest honey.

H: 45cm (18in); **S**: 50cm (20in)
❄❄❄ ◌ ☼ ♀

Ceanothus 'Blue Cushion'

This dwarf California lilac bears a mass of bright blue flowers in clusters all along its branches from mid- to late summer. It has glossy, evergreen leaves, and requires a warm, moderately sheltered, well-drained site, where it will rapidly spread.

H: 45cm (18in); **S**: 1m (3ft)
❄❄❄ ◌ ☼ ☀

Ceratostigma plumbaginoides
Perfect for rock gardens and as ground cover in warm, sheltered sites, this spreading subshrub bears masses of tiny, bright blue flowers in late summer. The mid-green oval leaves are carried on reddish stems; foliage becomes red-tinted in autumn.

H: 45cm (18in); **S**: 1.2m (4ft)
❀❀❀ ◊ ☼ ♀

Chamaemelum nobile 'Treneague'
This is the best variety for use in a chamomile lawn as it is non-flowering. Its finely divided, feathery leaves make an attractive, fragrant, evergreen carpet. The plants knit together by sending out sideshoots, which form rosettes.

H: 15cm (6in); **S**: 30cm (12in)
❀❀❀ ◊ ☼ ♀

Cotoneaster dammeri
A great plant for year-round interest, this vigorous, spreading shrub makes effective ground cover when grown under taller plants. It has attractive, evergreen foliage with small, white flowers in early summer followed by masses of red berries in autumn.

H: 20cm (8in); **S**: 2m (6ft)
❀❀❀ ◊ ◗ ☼ ◐ ♀

Erica carnea 'Vivellii'
When planted in groups this is an excellent ground cover heather, with attractive, dark green, needle-like foliage tinged with purple and pink to magenta tubular flowers. This is a popular choice for sunny, exposed sites with light, acidic soil.

H: 20cm (8in); **S**: 35cm (14in)
❀❀❀ ◊ ☼ ♀

Euonymus fortunei 'Emerald 'n' Gold'
This evergreen shrub is grown for its spectacular bright green, oval leaves with striking golden edges. It has a scrambling habit but can also be trained to climb upwards if given support. Its flowers are insignificant.

H: 60cm (24in); **S**: 1m (3ft)
❀❀❀ ◊ ◗ ☼ ◐ ♀

Euphorbia polychroma
This evergreen perennial forms a rounded clump of attractive mid-green foliage and produces clusters of lime-green flowers in spring. Spurge is a great filler for spring-flowering borders but beware of the milky sap, which can irritate skin.

H: 40cm (16in); **S**: 60cm (24in)
❀❀❀ ◊ ◗ ☼ ◐ ♀

Ground cover for sun *continued*

Genista hispanica

Spanish gorse produces yellow flowers and is densely packed with twigs and tiny green spines. Despite its evergreen appearance it is actually a deciduous shrub and benefits from hard pruning if it becomes too straggly. It thrives in warm sites.

H: 70cm (28in); **S**: 50cm (20in)
✽✽✽ ◊ ☼

Houttuynia cordata 'Flame'

A versatile ground-cover plant that thrives in both damp or well-drained soil, this vigorous, deciduous, fast-growing perennial has upright stems and impressive multi-coloured leaves. Insignificant sprays of small white flowers are produced in summer.

H: 35cm (14in); **S**: 1m (3ft)
✽✽✽ ◊ ◊ ◊ ☼ ☀

Hypericum calycinum

A valuable and quickly spreading ground-cover plant, rose of Sharon provides interest over many seasons thanks to its attractive foliage and long flowering period. It produces bright yellow, star-shaped blooms with impressive red-tipped anthers.

H: 60cm (24in); **S**: 1.5m (5ft)
✽✽✽ ◊ ◊ ☼ ☀

Juniperus horizontalis

Creeping juniper is a prostrate, evergreen shrub with a spreading habit; it forms an attractive carpet of grey-green foliage that turns purplish in winter. It is a useful plant for covering difficult areas such as steep banks where mowers cannot reach.

H: 35cm (14in); **S**: 2.5m (8ft)
✽✽✽ ◊ ☼ ☀

Luzula nivea

An evergreen, tufted, ornamental grass-like perennial, snowy woodrush makes great ground cover for both shady sites or in full sun. It produces a profusion of pale white flowers from early to midsummer, which can be dried and used in flower displays.

H: 60cm (24in); **S**: 45cm (18in)
✽✽✽ ◊ ◊ ☼ ☀

Mentha requienii

An interesting alternative to chamomile or thyme when creating a scented, non-grass lawn, Corsican mint produces a mass of tiny, very aromatic leaves that smell of peppermint. It also bears tiny, purple flowers in late summer.

H: 15cm (6in); **S**: 45cm (18in)
✽✽✽ ◊ ◊ ☼ ☀

Nepeta 'Six Hills Giant'

Called catmint because cats seem to love rolling in it, this plant bears mint-like, greyish, aromatic leaves and produces a profusion of bright blue flowers. It thrives in arid, infertile, and well-drained soils, and is attractive to bees and butterflies.

H: 45cm (18in); **S**: 45cm (18in)
❁❁❁ ◊ ☼

Origanum vulgare 'Aureum'

Golden marjoram has highly aromatic leaves that can be used in cooking. An ideal ground cover for a sunny bank or in a herb garden, this bushy perennial produces tiny golden-yellow leaves and small pink flowers in summer.

H: 30cm (12in); **S**: 30cm (12in)
❁❁❁ ◊ ☼ ♈

Persicaria bistorta 'Superba'

This fast-growing semi-evergreen produces dense, cylindrical, pink flowerheads from early summer through to autumn, held high above dock leaf-like foliage. It is a vigorous plant and may need regular cutting back to keep it to size.

H: 70cm (28in); **S**: 1m (3ft)
❁❁❁ ◊ ◑ ● ☼ ◔ ♈

Phlomis russeliana

This striking, upright, herbaceous perennial produces hooded, pale yellow flowers along its stem from late spring right through into late autumn. The foliage is pointed, hairy, and mid-green and grows in opposite pairs along the stem.

H: 1m (3ft); **S**: 75cm (30in)
❁❁❁ ◊ ☼ ◔ ♈

Rosmarinus officinalis 'Severn Sea'

A popular culinary and medicinal herb, rosemary is an evergreen shrub bearing small, dark blue flowers in summer. The foliage is dark green and needle-like, borne on arching stems. Native to the Mediterranean, it prefers light, sandy soils.

H: 60cm (24in); **S**: 60cm (24in)
❁❁❁ ◊ ☼ ♈

Stachys byzantina

Commonly known as lambs' ears or bunnies' ears due to the soft, velvety texture of its leaves, this plant produces small tubular pink flowers on white, woolly upright stems in summer. The foliage is evergreen, thick, and very hairy.

H: 30cm (12in); **S**: 60cm (24in)
❁❁❁ ◊ ☼

Ground cover for dry shade

Ajuga reptans
A creeping, semi-evergreen perennial, bugle has glossy, rosette-shaped, dark green foliage, although there are varieties with crimson, purple, and bronze leaves. In early summer, short blue or white flower spikes provide an interesting contrast to the leaves.

H: 15cm (6in); **S**: 60cm (24in)
❀❀❀ ◊ ◗ ☼

Arctostaphylos uva-ursi
Bear berry is a low-growing, evergreen shrub which bears shiny, dark green leaves that take on a striking bronze hue in autumn. It bears small, bell-shaped, pink flowers in spring followed by deep red berries. It requires acid soil for successful growth.

H: 20cm (8in); **S**: 3m (9ft)
❀❀❀ ◊ ◗ ☼

Asplenium scolopendrium
An upright and evergreen perennial, hart's tongue fern is ideal for covering steep, shady banks when planted *en masse*. It has green, tongue-shaped, leathery fronds – the rust-coloured spores are arranged in a herringbone pattern on the underside.

H: 50cm (20in); **S**: 60cm (24in)
❀❀❀ ◊ ◗ ☼ ♈

Bergenia cordifolia 'Purpurea'
This classic evergreen perennial for shady borders is known as elephant's ears for its large, rounded, deep green leaves that turn purplish in autumn. It has a clump-forming habit and bears pink, bell-shaped flowers on reddish stems in late winter and early spring.

H: 45cm (18in); **S**: 50cm (20in)
❀❀❀ ◊ ◗ ☼ ♈

Brunnera macrophylla
This spring-flowering perennial bears large, pointed heart-shaped leaves up to 15cm (6in) long and upright clusters of pale blue flowers, similar to forget-me-nots. A fast-spreading plant, it looks good when planted around taller shrubs or under trees.

H: 45cm (18in); **S**: 60cm (24in)
❀❀❀ ◊ ◗ ☼ ♈

Cyclamen hederifolium
This autumn-flowering, tuberous perennial has impressive pale to deep pink flowers, each with a deep red flush at its mouth. The foliage, which is ivy-like in shape with green and silver mottling, appears after the flowers. It requires fertile soil.

H: 15cm (6in); **S**: 15cm (6in)
❀❀❀ ◊ ◗ ☼ ☀ ♈

Galium odoratum

A useful ground-cover plant for poor soil, sweet woodruff is a vigorous, mat-forming perennial that provides a carpet of bright green, lance-shaped leaves in woodland gardens and shady borders. Clusters of white, starry flowers appear in spring.

H: 40cm (16in); **S**: 1.5m (5ft)
❅❅❅ ◊ ◗ ☼ ☀

Hedera helix 'Glacier'

A useful wildlife plant for both birds and insects, 'Glacier' has impressive triangular green leaves, with attractive grey-green and cream variegation. An evergreen woodland plant, this ivy can be used either as ground cover or as a climber.

H: 1.5m (5ft); **S**: 1.5m (5ft)
❅❅❅ ◊ ◗ ☼ ☀ ♀

Lamium maculatum 'White Nancy'

Mat-forming, herbaceous deadnettle can be invasive, so check it regularly and keep it away from neighbouring smaller plants. It produces pure white flowers and its semi-evergreen leaves are silver with green margins.

H: 20cm (8in); **S**: 1m (3ft)
❅❅❅ ◗ ☼ ☀ ♀

Luzula sylvatica 'Aurea'

This rampant ground-cover plant is native to shady woodlands and invaluable for steep banks where mowing would be impossible. It is a tough, evergreen, tufted perennial with insignificant, pale white flowers and clumps of bright golden foliage.

H: 60cm (24in); **S**: 45cm (18in)
❅❅❅ ◗ ☼

Nandina domestica

An attractive evergreen or semi-evergreen shrub, heavenly bamboo has red foliage when young, which matures to green, turning red again in autumn. In warm areas, small white flowers are borne in midsummer, followed by red berries.

H: 2m (6ft); **S**: 1.5m (5ft)
❅❅❅ ◗ ☼ ♀

Pachysandra terminalis

This bushy, spreading, evergreen foliage plant is ideal for a woodland garden or shady shrub border. It has oval, dark green leaves that appear in whorls at the end of its stems. The white flowers are borne in small spikes in early summer.

H: 20cm (8in); **S**: 3m (9ft)
❅❅❅ ◗ ☼ ☀

Ground cover for dry shade *continued*

Pulmonaria 'Blue Ensign'

With their unusual speckled foliage, *Pulmonaria* are popular ground-cover plants for underplanting shrub borders and planting in light woodlands; 'Blue Ensign' is distinctive as its grey-green foliage is speckle-free. It bears bright blue flowers.

H: 30cm (12in); **S**: 30cm (12in)
❄❄❄ ◊ ◐ ☼ ☀

Sarcococca ruscifolia

Known as sweet box, this slow-growing, evergreen shrub has foliage reminiscent of the box plant (*Buxus*). It has a suckering habit and makes a useful ground-cover plant when established. It produces small, white, powerfully fragrant flowers in winter.

H: 10cm (4in); **S**: 1m (3ft)
❄❄❄ ◊ ◐ ☼ ☀

Symphytum 'Goldsmith'

Comfrey is a robust plant with coarse, dark green leaves that are edged and splashed with gold and cream. The tubular flowers are pale blue and appear in early summer. The leaves can be chopped up and added to water to create a liquid feed.

H: 60cm (24in); **S**: 60cm (24in)
❄❄❄ ◐ ☼

Tiarella wherryi

A popular woodland plant, the foam flower bears attractive three-lobed, purple-tinged foliage and spikes of small whitish-pink flowers in spring and early summer. It prefers humus-rich soil and is ideal for planting under taller shrubs or shady borders.

H: 50cm (20in); **S**: 50cm (20in)
❄❄❄ ◊ ◐ ☼ ☀ ♈

Vinca minor

Considered by some to be a weed due to its spreading nature, periwinkle bears attractive dark violet flowers throughout summer and dark green foliage. It is a useful plant for steep banks or bare ground under trees. It is an excellent weed suppressant.

H: 50cm (20in); **S**: 2m (6ft)
❄❄❄ ◊ ◐ ☼ ☀

Waldsteinia ternata

This creeping evergreen plant forms a thick, dense carpet, ideal for suppressing weeds. It has serrated, lobed foliage similar to that of strawberries and in late spring and early summer produces pretty single, bright yellow flowers.

H: 10cm (4in); **S**: 60cm (24in)
❄❄❄ ◊ ◐ ☼ ☀

Ground cover for damp shade

Convallaria majalis

This creeping, herbaceous perennial fills the air with its beautiful fragrance during late spring and early summer. Lily-of-the-valley produces clusters of fragrant, white, bell-shaped flowers held high over narrow, oval, mid- to dark green foliage.

H: 25cm (10in); **S**: 30cm (12in)
❋❋❋ ◌ ☼ ☀ ♛

Cornus canadensis

Creeping dogwood is an excellent choice for underplanting shrubs in acidic, woodland conditions. The oval, bright green leaves are deeply veined and the flowers appear in clusters with prominent white bracts during spring and summer, followed by red berries.

H: 15cm (6in); **S**: 3m (9ft)
❋❋❋ ◌ ☼ ☀ ♛

Hosta 'Sum and Substance'

A moist shade-loving plant, this hosta is ideal for the dappled shade in woodlands or near the edges of ponds. It has lush, decorative, golden-green foliage and trumpet-shaped, pale lavender flower spikes. Protect the plants against slugs.

H: 1m (3ft); **S**: 1m (3ft)
❋❋❋ ◌ ☼ ☀ ♛

Pratia pedunculata

This useful Australian plant thrives in both full sun or deep shade although it does prefer moist soil. It produces masses of deep green evergreen leaves and the creeping stems are covered with pale violet flowers throughout the summer.

H: 50cm (20in); **S**: 1.3m (4½ft)
❋❋❋ ◌ ◌ ☼ ☼ ☀

Rubus tricolor

This evergreen ornamental bramble originates from China and has a spreading habit that will quickly colonize an area. It is called "tricolor" because of its three colours: the glossy-green foliage, white summer flowers, and red fruit in autumn.

H: 60cm (24in); **S**: 3m (9ft)
❋❋❋ ◌ ◌ ☼ ☀

Soleirolia soleirolii

A prostrate evergreen, mind-your-own-business forms a carpet of dense green foliage with its tiny leaves and insignificant flowers. It spreads rapidly in moist soils in mild areas, covering rocks as well as soil. It can become slightly weedy.

H: 10cm (4in); **S**: 1m (3ft)
❋❋❋ ◌ ☼

Suppliers

Many of these suppliers are specialist nurseries, so it is worth checking the opening hours before visiting, especially if you are making a long journey.

For further information see the RHS website: www.rhs.org.uk.

Turf

Grasslands Nursery
Free Green Lane
Lower Peover
Knutsford
Cheshire
WA16 9QY
01565 723831
www.grasslands.co.uk

Online Turf
Mickering Lane
Aughton
Near Ormskirk
Lancashire
L39 6SR
0871 222 2522
www.onlineturf.co.uk

Rolawn
Elvington
York
YO41 4XR
0845 604 6050
01904 608661
www.rolawn.co.uk

The Sports Turf Research Institute
St Ives Estate
Bingley
West Yorkshire
BD16 1AU
01274 565131
www.stri.co.uk

Turf Shop
Tillers Turf Company Ltd
Grange Lane
North Kelsey
Lincolnshire
LN7 6EZ
www.turfshop.co.uk

Turf Supplies Direct
Guide Street
Weaste
Salford
M50 1BX
www.turfsuppliesdirect.co.uk

Ornamental grass

The Alpine and Grass Nursery
Northgate
West Pinchbeck
Spalding
Lincolnshire
PE11 3TB
01775 640935
www.alpinesandgrasses.co.uk

The Big Grass Company
Hookhill Plantation
Woolfardisworthy East
Nr Crediton
Devon
EX17 4RX
01363 866146

Bridge Nursery
Tomlow Road
Napton
Nr Rugby
Warwickshire
CV47 8HX
01926 812737
www.bridge-nursery.co.uk

Fordmouth Croft Ornamental Grass Nursery
Fordmouth Croft
Meikle Wartle
Inverurie
Aberdeenshire
AB51 5BE
01467 671519

Hall Farm Nursery
Vicarage Lane
Kinnerley
Nr Oswestry
Shropshire
SY10 8DH
01691 682135
www.hallfarmnursery.co.uk

Knoll Gardens
Hampreston
Wimborne
Dorset
BH21 7ND
01202 873931
www.knollgardens.co.uk

Artificial grass

Artificial grass
Tavistock Works
Glasson Industrial Estate
Maryport
Cumbria
CA15 8NT
01900 811970
www.artificial-grass.com

Easigrass™
Old Railway Yard
Lionel Road South
Brentford
London
TW8 0JA
08450 948880
www.easigrass.com

Evergreens UK
Exton Block
Market Overton Industrial Estate
Ironstone Lane
Rutland
LE15 7TP
01572 768208
www.evergreensuk.com

Express Grass
174–188 High Street
Sheerness
Kent
ME12 1UQ
0844 855 4704
www.expressgrass.com

Nomow
Unit 8 Colebrook Industrial Estate
Longfield Road
Tunbridge Wells
Kent
TN2 3DG
0800 587 0380
www.nomow.co.uk

Meadow seed mixtures

Chiltern Seeds
Bortree Stile
Ulverston
Cumbria
LA12 7PB
01229 581137
www.chilternseeds.co.uk

Emorsgate Seeds
Limes Farm
Tilney All Saints
King's Lynn
Norfolk
PE34 4RT
01553 829028
www.wildseed.co.uk

Landlife Wildflowers
National Wildflower Centre
Court Hey Park
Liverpool
L16 3NA
01517 371819
www.wildflower.org.uk

Pictorial Meadows
Manor Oaks Farmhouse
389 Manor Lane
Sheffield
S2 1UL
01142 677635
www.pictorialmeadows.co.uk

Really Wild Flowers
H.V. Horticulture Ltd.
55 Balcombe Road
Haywards Heath
West Sussex
RH16 1PE
01444 413376
www.reallywildflowers.co.uk

Ground cover and bulbs

Bloms Bulbs
Primrose Nurseries
Melchbourne
Bedfordshire
MK44 1ZZ
01234 709099
www.blomsbulbs.com

de Jager bulbs
Church Farm
Ulcombe
Maidstone
Kent
ME17 1DN
01622 840229
www.dejager.co.uk

Dobies of Devon
Long Road
Paignton
Devon
TQ4 7SX
Customer services: 0844 701 7623
Orderphone: 0844 701 7625
www.dobies.co.uk

D. T. Brown
Bury Road
Newmarket
CB8 7PQ
0845 371 0532
www.dtbrownseeds.co.uk

Gee Tee Bulb Company
Field Works
Common Road
Moulton Seas End
Spalding
Lincolnshire
PE12 6LF
01205 260412
www.gee-tee.co.uk

Suttons Seeds
Woodview Road
Paignton
Devon
TQ4 7NG
Customer services: 0844 922 2899
Orderphone: 0844 922 0606
www.suttons.co.uk

Thompson & Morgan
Poplar Lane
Ipswich
Suffolk
IP8 3BU
0844 248 5383
www.thompson-morgan.com

Victoriana Nursery Gardens
Challock
Nr Ashford
Kent
TN25 4DG
01233 740529
www.victoriananursery.co.uk

Index

Index

Acknowledgments

The publisher would like to thank the following for their kind permission to reproduce their photographs:

(Key: a-above; b-below/bottom; c-centre; f-far; l-left; r-right; t-top)

8 GAP Photos: Charles Hawes (tr). **9 Photolibrary:** Allan Mandell (bc). **10 Photolibrary:** Brian Carter (c). **11 GAP Photos:** Elke Borkowski (cr). **Photolibrary:** Zave Smith (tr). **12–13 Easigrass.com** (c). **13 As Good as Grass:** (cr). **Evergreens (UK) Ltd:** (br). **GAP Photos:** Brian North (tr). **14–15 GAP Photos:** Leigh Clapp. **15 Marianne Majerus Garden Images:** MMGI (tl). **18–19 GAP Photos:** Hanneke Reijbroek. **24 Marianne Majerus Garden Images:** MMGI (c). **25 The Garden Collection:** Jonathan Buckley (tr). **27 GAP Photos:** Lynn Keddie (br). **36 Photolibrary:** Suzie Gibbons (bl). **45 Getty Images:** Evan Sklar (bc, br). **51 Corbis:** Fritz Polking; Frank Lane Picture Agency (tc). **55 Peter Anderson:** (bc). **57 Garden World Images:** Eric Crichton (br). **58 GAP Photos:** Jo Whitworth (c). **60 GAP Photos:** Marcus Harpur (c). **69 The Garden Collection:** Jonathan Buckley (c). **71 The Garden Collection:** Nicola Stocken Tomkins (c). **73 The Garden Collection:** Derek Harris (c). **74 GAP Photos:** Dianna Jazwinski (br). **82 GAP Photos:** Adrian Bloom (br); Heather Edwards (cr); Fiona McLeod (cb). **86 GAP Photos:** Elke Borkowski (c). **89 GAP Photos:** Gerald Majumdar (c). **90 DK Images:** Rebecca Tennant (tr). **106 DK Images:** Caroline Reed (br). **107 DK Images:** Rebecca Tennant. **112 FLPA:** Nigel Cattlin (crb). **Royal Horticultural Society:** (cb). **Science Photo Library:** Nigel Cattlin (clb). **113 Corbis:** Wally Eberhart / Visuals Unlimited (cra). **DK Images:** Caroline Reed (tl). **GAP Photos:** FhF Greenmedia (cb); Flora Press (ca). **Science Photo Library:** Nigel Cattlin (clb). **116 Emorsgate Seeds:** (cl, c, cra, crb). **117 NHPA / Photoshot:** Liam Grant (cb). **Science Photo Library:** Wolfgang Hoffmann (ca). **The Sports Turf Research Institute:** (clb). **118 Emorsgate Seeds:** (ca, cra, cb). **FLPA:** Peter Wilson (clb). **119 Garden World Images:** Nigel Downer (ca). **120 GAP Photos:** Sarah Cuttle (cr). **Garden World Images:** Andrea Jones (ca). **121 GAP Photos:** Martin Hughes-Jones (cb); Howard Rice (cra). **122 Garden World Images:** (ca). **123 Corbis:** Niall Benvie (cb). **124 Corbis:** George McCarthy (ca). **125 Corbis:** Michael Maconachie; Papilio (cla); Ian Rose; Frank Lane Picture Agency (crb). **Garden World Images:** (cb). **126 Corbis:** Gary Meszaros / Visuals Unlimited (cla). **Garden World Images:** Martin Hughes-Jones (cra). **127 GAP Photos:** John Glover (cb); Jo Whitworth (cla). **Getty Images:** Richard Bloom (cra). **128 Corbis:** Harpur Garden Library (cla). **Getty Images:** Kelly Kalhoefer (cra). **133 Garden World Images:** (cb). **134 GAP Photos:** Matt Anker (cla). **136 GAP Photos:** Christina Bollen (cla). **Garden World Images:** (ca). **137 GAP Photos:** Howard Rice (cb). **Garden World Images:** Trevor Sims (cra)

All other images © Dorling Kindersley

For further information see: **www.dkimages.com**

Dorling Kindersley would also like to thank the following:
Alex Storch, Emorsgate Seeds, The Sports Turf Research Institute, Evergreens UK, Easigrass™, and Tony Wagstaff, designer of The Home Front garden created in association with Southend Youth Offending Service.

Photoshoot direction: Alison Gardner
Editorial assistance: Fiona Wild
Index: Jane Coulter